access to history

Hitler, Appeasement and the Road to War 1933–41 SECOND EDITION

Graham Darby

D1302911

HODDER
EDUCATION
AN HACHETTE UK COMPANY

The publishers would like to thank the following individuals, institutions and companies for permission to reproduce copyright illustrations in this book: Akg-images, pages 28, 51, 59; Akg-images/Ullstein Bild, page 41; © Bettmann/CORBIS, pages 24, 42, 135; © BPK, pages 38 (bottom), 61; © Hulton-Deutsch Collection/CORBIS, pages 11, 25 (bottom), 37, 58, 102, 129; Will Dyson, *Daily Herald* 13th May 1919/ British Cartoon Archive, University of Kent/Mirror Syndication International, page 92; David Low, *Evening Standard* 4th October 1935/British Cartoon Archive, University of Kent/Solo Syndication, page 35; David Low, *Evening Standard* 8 July 1936/British Cartoon Archive, University of Kent/Solo Syndication, page 45; David Low, *Evening Standard* 18 February 1938/British Cartoon Archive, University of Kent/Solo Syndication, page 75; David King Collection, pages 131, 134; Political Cartoon Society/*Daily Worker/Morning Star*, page 104; © Popperfoto.com, page 81; Reproduced with permission of Punch Ltd., www.punch.co.uk, pages 9, 38 (top), 54, 62 (bottom), 105.

The publishers would also like to thank the following for permission to reproduce material in this book: AQA Material is reproduced by permission of the Assessment and Qualifications Alliance, extracts used on pages 86, 144, 146; Edexcel Limited for extracts used on pages 47, 67, 88, 147; Oxford, Cambridge and RSA (OCR) examinations for extracts used on pages 115, 118, 121.

The publishers would like to acknowledge use of the following extracts: Addison Wesley Publishing Company for an extract from *The Origins of the Second World War* by P. Bell, 1997; Cambridge University Press for an extract from *The Origins of the First and Second World Wars* by F. McDonough, 1997; Harcourt for an extract from *Churchill: The End of Glory* by John Charmley, 1993; Hodder Arnold (H&S) for an extract from *Hitler – Germany's Fate or Germany's Misfortune* by J. Laver, 1995; Houghton Mifflin Co. for an extract from *Mein Kampf* by A. Hitler; Houghton Mifflin Co. for an extract from *Winston Churchill, Volume V: 1922–1939* by M. Gilbert, 1976; Humanity Books for an extract from *The Continental Commitment* by M. Howard, 1972; Longman Publishing Group for an extract from *Origins of the Second World War* by R.J. Overy, 1987; Macmillan & Co. Ltd. for an extract from *Diplomatic Prelude 1938–9* by L.B. Namier, 1948; Manchester University Press for an extract from *Neville Chamberlain* by F. McDonough, 1998; Oxford University Press for extracts from *English History 1914–45* by A.J.P. Taylor, 1965; Palgrave Macmillan for an extract from *Chamberlain & Appeasement* by R.A.C. Parker, 1993; Pantheon for an extract from *How War Came* by D. Watt, 1989; Routledge for an extract from *The Origins of the Second World War* by R. Henig, 1985; Touchstone Books for an extract from *The Origins of the Second World War* by A.J.P. Taylor, 1961; Weidenfeld & Nicholson for an extract from *Churchill: A Study in Failure* by R.R. James, 1970; W.W. Norton & Co. Inc. for an extract from *British Appeasement in the 1930's* by William Rock, 1977.

Every effort has been made to trace and acknowledge ownership of copyright. The publishers will be glad to make suitable arrangements with any copyright holders whom it has not been possible to contact.

Orders: please contact Bookpoint Ltd, 130 Milton Park, Abingdon, Oxon OX14 4SB. Telephone: (44) 01235 827720. Fax: (44) 01235 400454. Lines are open 9.00–5.00, Monday to Saturday, with a 24-hour message answering service. Visit our website at www.hoddereducation.co.uk

© Graham Darby 2007
First published in 2007 by
Hodder Education,
an Hachette UK Company,
338 Euston Road
London NW1 3BH

Impression number	5 4
Year	2011 2010 2009

Cover photo Ullstein Bild – Walter Frentz
Typeset in Baskerville 10/12pt and produced by Gray Publishing, Tunbridge Wells
Printed in Malta

A catalogue record for this title is available from the British Library

ISBN-13: 978 0340 929 285

Contents

Chapter 6 The Outbreak of War

Chapter 7 War

Chapter 8 Conclusion

Dedication

Keith Randell (1943–2002)

The *Access to History* series was conceived and developed by Keith, who created a series to 'cater for students as they are, not as we might wish them to be'. He leaves a living legacy of a series that for over 20 years has provided a trusted, stimulating and well-loved accompaniment to post-16 study. Our aim with these new editions is to continue to offer students the best possible support for their studies.

1 Introduction

POINTS TO CONSIDER

This chapter will introduce you to the historiography of the causes of the Second World War and some of the key questions that have been generated. It will then go on to give you an overview of the book's content and an outline of the period 1919–33. Your aim will be to keep the key questions in mind as well as the important events of 1919–33 which form the context for the later years. The key areas examined are:

- The historians' debate
- An overview of the book's content
- The weaknesses of the Paris Peace Settlement
- Keeping the peace
- Economic collapse and diplomatic instability

Key dates

1919	June 28	Paris Peace Settlement
1921		Reparations fixed at 132 billion gold marks (£6.6 million)
1922	April 16	Treaty of Rapallo between Germany and the USSR
1923	January 11	French occupation of the Ruhr (to 27 August 1925)
1924	April 9	Dawes Plan
1925	December 1	Treaty of Locarno
1926	September 10	Germany joined the League of Nations
1927	January 31	Rearmament no longer subject to scrutiny
1929	June 7	Young Plan
	October 29	Wall Street Crash
1930	June 30	Allied evacuation of the Rhineland
1931	September 18	Japan invaded Manchuria
1932	February	Disarmament Conference
	July 9	Reparations effectively abolished
1933	January 30	Hitler became Chancellor
	March	Japan left the League of Nations

1 | The Historians' Debate

Early certainty

The explanation for the origins of the Second World War used to be a relatively straightforward matter: the (innocent) Western democracies had been attacked by a ruthless, expansionist Germany. Unlike the First World War, where there was considerable scope for debate about origins and responsibility, the Second World War seemed easily explained. Germany provoked the war to reverse the verdict of the last one, destroy the Treaty of Versailles and win continental hegemony. More than that, the conflict was largely due to one man, the German Chancellor and leader of the Nazi Party, Adolf Hitler. He and his cronies planned the war and brought it about. Accordingly, this was the principal charge brought against captured Nazis at the **Nuremberg Trials** in 1946 – that they had conspired to bring about an aggressive war.

Lost opportunities?

So, in the light of this diagnosis, was the Second World War inevitable? Perhaps, perhaps not – there was also an alternative explanation. For despite Hitler's ruthless determination, was it conceivably a war that could have been avoided, an 'unnecessary war', in the words of Winston Churchill? Part of this argument was a list of 'lost opportunities' to stop Hitler; for instance, when he **remilitarised** the Rhineland in 1936 (see page 36), or at Munich in 1938 when he was given part of Czechoslovakia (see page 76).

Had Chamberlain not appeased, had France been more decisive, had the Soviet Union not collaborated, had the USA not been **isolationist**, then, the argument went, the war would have been less likely to occur. But occur it did, and this speculation did not alter the picture that much: Hitler was still responsible. The avoidable war and the inevitable war could be reconciled. Hitler planned the war, so the argument goes, but the democracies did play a part in failing to stop him. Thus, what was avoidable at one time became inevitable later.

The Taylor controversy

Although there was not always complete consensus, these explanations by and large held sway until A.J.P. Taylor turned everything upside down with his book *The Origins of the Second World War* in 1961. Taylor saw Hitler not as an evil monster bent on world domination, but as an ordinary German statesman whose policy was not dissimilar to that of his predecessors. At the same time, the German historian Fritz Fischer also stressed the continuity of aims between the **Second and Third Reichs**,

Key question
How have historians' views on the origins of the Second World War changed over time?

Key terms

Nuremberg Trials
Nuremberg was the scene of war trials in which a number of leading Nazis were tried by a military tribunal between 1945 and 1949.

Remilitarisation
Soldiers being sent back into an area where they had been banned.

Isolationist
A reference to US policy that involved non-participation in or withdrawal from international affairs.

Second and Third Reichs
Reich means empire in German. The Second refers to Germany between 1871 and 1918; the Third refers to Hitler's Germany 1933–45.

Key question
How did A.J.P. Taylor stir up debate?

September Programme
A set of war aims drawn up by the German Chancellor Bethmann Hollweg in September 1914, which envisaged annexations to create a German-dominated middle Europe.

Treaty of Brest-Litovsk
Imposed on Russia in March 1918 whereby a vast amount of Russian territory was annexed, albeit for a short time, including Poland and Lithuania.

Raison d'état
What was best for the state.

Appeasement
Pacification; in this context the policy of conciliating a potential aggressor by making concessions.

Lebensraum
'Living space': this refers to Hitler's desire for land in the east.

Hossbach Memorandum
The record of a meeting that took place in 1937 in which Hitler outlined his future plans for territorial acquisition and war.

comparing Bethmann Hollweg's **September Programme** and the **Treaty of Brest-Litovsk** with Hitler's writings. For Taylor the Second World War was not so much Hitler's war as a re-run of 1914–18. It was a case of old-fashioned balance-of-power politics, in which the powers vied with each other in a struggle for the mastery of Europe.

Moreover, Britain and France were not wholly innocent; they too were governed by *raison d'état* rather than moral considerations: they were equally self-interested. Thus, if British and French policies were self-serving, then in this context **appeasement**, the much criticised policy of making concessions, also took on a different light – perhaps it was the most appropriate policy at the time and a way of buying time (the debate on appeasement will be dealt with in Chapter 5). And it must be remembered that Britain and France declared war on Germany, not the other way round.

Opportunist or planner?

Central to Taylor's thesis was his belief that Hitler was simply an opportunist and not a planner. Responding to this contention, Alan Bullock in the second edition of his biography of Hitler (1962) confirmed Hitler's opportunism, but also highlighted his plans to overthrow Versailles and achieve German domination of Europe. He resolved this apparent contradiction by seeing him as an opportunist in the short term, but a planner in the long term.

Still others preferred to see Hitler solely as a planner and ascribed to him a blueprint for action (e.g. William Shirer in his bestseller of 1960, *The Rise and Fall of the Third Reich*), a contention borne out by the regularity of his moves, the systematic way he went from one demand to another (each being 'positively my last' … !). Hugh Trevor Roper suggested that Hitler's planning went beyond Versailles and hegemony: *lebensraum* was his fundamental aim, and this required a war of conquest. However, Taylor saw only opportunism and dismissed the idea of any plan at all. The **Hossbach Memorandum** (1937) for instance, he described as 'day-dreaming' (see page 69): 'there was no concrete plan', was his conclusion.

Taylor's book caused quite a stir at the time, generating more vitriol than endorsement, but it did spawn debate, a new look at the origins of the war, an end to complacency and a plethora of new research and writing which made it clear that the picture was really more complex than had been thought hitherto.

Intentionalists and functionalists

Subsequently, in the late 1960s, historians began to divide into two schools of thought, the **intentionalists** on the one hand and **functionalists/structuralists** on the other.

Key question
How do these historians differ?

The intentionalists

For the intentionalists Hitler remains central to the origins of the war. Many identify a clear intention to wage war based on the ideas of racial supremacy and the acquisition of a German world empire outlined in his writings. But whether or not you subscribe to the idea that Hitler had a plan, it was still, according to this school of thought, his dictatorial will that was the determining factor in the foreign policy of the Third Reich, in the drive to war. Intentionalists include the historians Klaus Hildebrand, Andreas Hillgruber and Eberhard Jäckel.

The functionalists

Functionalists, on the other hand, believe that foreign policy was created by the economic and social conditions of the Third Reich: it was determined by the structure of the state, and that structure was an anarchy of competing agencies. Hitler was in fact a weak dictator and the Nazi administration was chaotic; hence Nazi policy was reactive. This harked back to Taylor. Hans Mommsen reiterated the fact that Hitler had no plan and Martin Broszat saw *lebensraum* not as a concrete goal but as an ideological metaphor – an image to aim for, to justify unceasing foreign policy initiatives.

Tim Mason contended that the war occurred as a result of the domestic, economic crisis in Germany in the late 1930s. He stated that, by June 1941, 'it was clear that the German war economy would have collapsed in 1939/40 if the occupied areas had not been looted of raw materials, foodstuffs, war ***matériel*** and production capacity'. Basically what he meant is that the German economy could not continue to expand or even function at the same capacity without plundering neighbouring states: Hitler had to expand the Reich to avoid economic disaster. Rearmament and the expense of public works could not be sustained indefinitely.

Intentionalists
Historians who believe that it was Hitler's intention to wage war.

Functionalists/structuralists
Two alternative terms for the same group of historians who believe that it was the structure of the state that created policy rather than a single man.

Matériel
Available means, especially materials and equipment in warfare.

Key terms

Conclusion

However, just as Taylor's work did not achieve acceptance (and has subsequently been shown to be flawed in a number of crucial areas) so too the functionalists have not really had the best of the debate. Although their researches have enriched our historical knowledge of the functioning of the Third Reich, there is difficulty in demonstrating how social and economic factors influenced the formation of foreign policy. Indeed there is hardly any evidence at all to show that they did. For most observers the intentionalists are more convincing and the title of this book is a reflection of that fact.

But if 'the centrality of Hitler and German policy to the origins of the war is little questioned by historians' (Crozier), there are nevertheless a number of key questions thrown up by all this historical debate, and ones which will have to be addressed in the course of this book.

Some key questions

- How much continuity was there between the foreign policies of the Second (1871–1918) and Third (1933–45) Reichs? Was Hitler little different from his predecessors? Were his aims the same as the Kaiser's in 1914? Or Stresemann's in the 1920s?
- Was Hitler an opportunist or a planner? Did he have a **blueprint**, a timetable which he followed? Did Nazi ideology make the war inevitable? Did Hitler get the war he wanted or did it come about by accident?
- Could Hitler have been stopped at any stage prior to 1939? Was the war avoidable?
- Did Hitler intend a series of short wars or a much larger war, starting in the 1940s? What do Nazi economic and rearmament policies tell us about his intentions?
- Who was morally responsible for the outbreak of the war? How much blame should be allotted to Hitler, to the Nazis, to the German people, to Britain, France, and the Soviet Union? In this context, was appeasement a cowardly policy that only encouraged Hitler? Or was it an honourable policy, or the only policy open to the democracies?

Key term

Blueprint
A detailed plan, especially in the early stages of a project or idea.

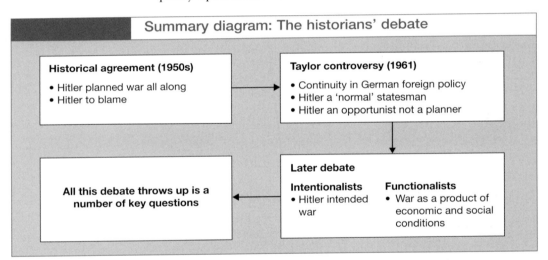

Summary diagram: The historians' debate

Historical agreement (1950s)
- Hitler planned war all along
- Hitler to blame

Taylor controversy (1961)
- Continuity in German foreign policy
- Hitler a 'normal' statesman
- Hitler an opportunist not a planner

Later debate

Intentionalists
- Hitler intended war

Functionalists
- War as a product of economic and social conditions

All this debate throws up is a number of key questions

Some key books in the debate

M. Broszat, *The Hitler State* (Longman, 1981).
A. Bullock, *Hitler: A Study in Tyranny* (Pelican, 1962).
W. Churchill, *The Gathering Storm* (originally 1948; Penguin, 2005).
A. Crozier, *The Causes of the Second World War* (Blackwell, 1997).
F. Fischer, *From Kaiserreich to Third Reich* (Routledge, 1991).
K. Hildebrand, *The Foreign Policy of the Third Reich* (Batsford, 1973).
A. Hillgruber, *Germany and the Two World Wars* (Harvard, 1981).
T. Mason, *Nazism, Fascism and the Working Class* (a collection of articles edited by Jane Caplan, CUP, 1995).
W. Mommsen, *The Third Reich between Vision and Reality* (Berg, 2003).
A. Taylor, *Origins of the Second World War* (Hamish Hamilton, 1961).

2 | An Overview of the Book's Content

This book will concentrate principally on the years 1933–39 and will look at all the major powers involved. However, given the centrality of Hitler's role, we will mainly focus on his actions and the reaction of the major powers to those actions.

Early years (Chapter 2)

Initially we will consider the origins and sources for Hitler's thinking, his writings and his speeches. We will look at the centrality of 'race' and 'space' in his foreign policy objectives. In the years 1933–6 his position was weak, but even so he was able to exploit allied disunity and accelerate rearmament, introduce **conscription**, remilitarise the Rhineland and even plan for war 4 years hence.

Diplomatic revolution (Chapter 3)

Something of a diplomatic revolution occurred between 1935 and 1937 as Mussolini, Italy's dictator, hitherto a potential ally of the democracies and wary of Hitler, was condemned for his attack on Abyssinia (now Ethiopia) by Britain and France and reacted by making a deal with the German dictator. The **League of Nations** was further discredited and Hitler took advantage of the situation to remilitarise the Rhineland (1936). The Spanish Civil War also brought the dictators closer together and the Rome–Berlin Axis was formed at the end of the year. Later, in 1939, it became a full military alliance, the **Pact of Steel**. This part of the book will look at the dictators' relations throughout the period 1933–9, during which time the Italian dictator, an established leader who was initially contemptuous of Hitler, came to be very much the junior partner, trailing in the German dictator's wake.

Hitler changes gear 1937–8 (Chapter 4)

Now the balance of power had been altered, Hitler began to take the initiative. The Hossbach Memorandum of 1937 should be seen in this context and should be taken seriously, contrary to A.J.P. Taylor's objections. The generals who objected were soon removed and there followed the *Anschluss* with Austria in March 1938. The timing was not Hitler's, but the democracies' acquiescence was a lesson not lost on the German dictator. The partition of Czechoslovakia, conceded by the democracies at Munich, followed in September.

Appeasement (Chapter 5)

Clearly Hitler increasingly took the initiative, but it is essential that students appreciate the problems faced by the democracies. France was not only affected by a strong strain of **pacifism**, but was in fact economically and militarily weak, and largely dependent on Britain. British policy was very much determined

Key question
What are the major issues under discussion in this book?

Key terms

Conscription
Compulsory enlistment for military service; forbidden by the Treaty of Versailles.

League of Nations
An association of countries established in 1919 by the Treaty of Versailles to promote international co-operation and achieve international peace and security.

Pact of Steel
A full military alliance between Germany and Italy signed in 1939.

Anschluss
German for 'joining'. Annexation – to incorporate or add territory to one's own.

Pacifism
The belief that war and violence are morally unjustified.

by its global commitments and global vulnerability. These considerations, taken together with a feeling of sympathy for some revision of Versailles, render British policy intelligible. Seen in this light, appeasement looks like a rational policy based on what was possible. However, it was only compromise up to a point, as the historiographical debate on Prime Minister Chamberlain will show.

The outbreak of war 1939 (Chapter 6)

After Munich, Hitler broke his promises and occupied the rest of Czechoslovakia. Britain and France's guarantees to Poland in March 1939 were intended to be a warning to Hitler to deter him from any future moves. Even before the occupation of Prague, Czechoslovakia's capital, a decision had been reached to draw a line in the sand; that is to say, it was decided that Hitler's demands should now be resisted. However, the democracies' antipathy towards Stalin enabled Hitler to pull off a remarkable **diplomatic coup** with the **Nazi–Soviet Pact** in August 1939. Hitler pressed ahead with his invasion of Poland on 1 September, convinced that he had avoided a general war.

War (Chapter 7)

Hitler, however, was wrong. But quite why Britain and France decided to make a stand at this point will be investigated. The war went badly for the democracies; Hitler won a rapid and remarkable victory in the west in the summer of 1940. However, for Hitler this military triumph was really only a sideshow. The main aim remained *lebensraum*, and **Operation Barbarossa** was the prelude to a new racial order, the triumph of the teuton (German) over the slav (the Russians). Arguably everything had been leading up to this point.

Conclusion (Chapter 8)

Accordingly, there is a very good case for laying the responsibility for the war at the feet of Hitler. However, it would be facile to blame just one man. Hitler was not operating in a vacuum; he was in fact operating in a most favourable climate, and it is to this broader context that we must now turn. Without defeat in the First World War, without the humiliation of Versailles and without the collapse of the world economy at the time of the Depression, it is inconceivable that Adolf Hitler could have come to power.

Key terms

Diplomatic coup
A successful move in international relations.

Nazi–Soviet Pact
An agreement between Germany and the USSR that contained a secret deal to partition Poland.

Operation Barbarossa
Hitler's invasion of the Soviet Union in the summer of 1941.

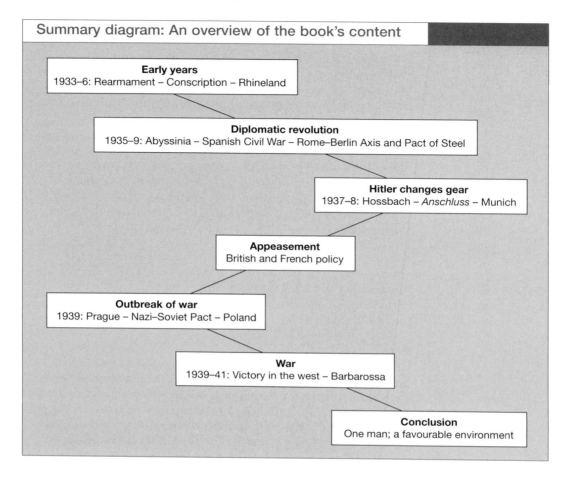

Summary diagram: An overview of the book's content

Early years
1933–6: Rearmament – Conscription – Rhineland

Diplomatic revolution
1935–9: Abyssinia – Spanish Civil War – Rome–Berlin Axis and Pact of Steel

Hitler changes gear
1937–8: Hossbach – *Anschluss* – Munich

Appeasement
British and French policy

Outbreak of war
1939: Prague – Nazi–Soviet Pact – Poland

War
1939–41: Victory in the west – Barbarossa

Conclusion
One man; a favourable environment

3 | The Weaknesses of the Paris Peace Settlement

Introduction

For many observers, the Second World War was a rerun of the First. Put simply, the side that had begun the conflict in 1914 lost, and tried to reverse that decision in 1939. Proponents of this view see the inadequacy of the Treaty of Versailles as fundamental, contending that the settlement fell between two stools, arguably too harsh and too soft at the same time.

November 1918

The collapse of the German war effort in November 1918 was sudden and unexpected, coming as a surprise to both the **Allies** and the German people. After all, earlier in the year, Russia had finally acknowledged defeat and the German army had launched a fresh offensive that had again taken its forces close to Paris: the German people anticipated victory. Although this offensive had failed by the summer and the Germans been pushed back, they had not been defeated and the Allies were making firm arrangements for 1919 and even talking of war lasting into 1920.

Key question
Why did the war's end come as a surprise?

Allies
Britain, France, the USA and those on their side.

Key term

Key terms

Wilson's 14 Points
A peace programme put forward by Woodrow Wilson, the US President, in January 1918.

Socialist
A person who believes that the means of production, distribution and exchange should be regulated or owned by the community as a whole.

Thus, the sudden end to the war in November 1918 caught everyone unprepared.

Indeed the way the war ended, with the German army intact and Germany unoccupied, served to hide what had really happened and led to false assumptions in Germany.

- First, there was the belief that the war had been ended by the Germans prematurely in order to obtain a soft peace based on **Wilson's 14 Points**.
- Secondly, when that peace turned out not to be soft, there developed the myth that the army had not been defeated at all but had been 'stabbed in the back' and betrayed by democratic and **socialist** politicians. The fact that both these assumptions are wrong is irrelevant because they do help to explain the German attitude to the peace settlement.

This cartoon from *Punch*, published in 1919, clearly advocated that Britain and France should take a tough line with the Germans.

GIVING HIM ROPE?

GERMAN CRIMINAL (*to Allied Police*). "HERE, I SAY, STOP! YOU'RE HURTING ME! [*Aside*]
IF I ONLY WHINE ENOUGH I MAY BE ABLE TO WRIGGLE OUT OF THIS YET."

The Treaty of Versailles

The suddenness of the end of war meant that the Treaty of Versailles was cobbled together and signed in great haste and confusion. In effect, it was the work of three men: President Wilson of the USA and the Prime Ministers of Britain and France, Lloyd George and Clemenceau. The portrayal of their positions as **idealism**, **pragmatism** and revenge, respectively, is undoubtedly an oversimplification, but it is nevertheless a useful characterisation. The 'Big Three' were under tremendous pressure and worked without an agenda, and with imperfect information, in a hectic 6-week period. They had to strike deals; they had to compromise. To suggest, as some commentators do, that the peacemakers faced appalling if not insurmountable difficulties, and did quite well in the circumstances might be a fair point to make, but it only serves to reinforce the judgement that it *was* an imperfect peace.

It is clear that the Treaty of Versailles was neither soft enough to reconcile the Germans, nor harsh enough to cripple them forever: it fell between two stools. It left Germany with grievances and the potential power to make trouble in the future. In fact it was felt to be a stunning blow to German pride.

German resentment

First of all the Germans resented the fact that the peace was a *diktat* – there was simply no time for consultation. The Germans had expected a negotiated settlement. They resented the entire peace, but in particular:

- The War Guilt Clause (Article 231), which stated that Germany was solely responsible for the outbreak of the war. Many historians now believe, as the peacemakers did then, that the Germans were responsible for the war (although, of course, the men of the Kaiser's government who had taken the decisions in 1914 were no longer in charge).
- The Germans had to pay reparations, although in truth the delay in fixing the amount (until 1921) worked in Germany's favour and only a trivial sum was ever paid.
- The Germans lost territory – 13 per cent of their land and 10 per cent of their population, as well as all their colonies – but the Germans themselves would have imposed a much harsher peace on their defeated enemies (their September Programme envisaged massive annexations) if they had won.
- The **principle of national self-determination** was adopted at the peace settlement for all peoples except Germans (millions of Germans were now in Poland and Czechoslovakia, and a further seven million in Austria). This simply served to regenerate and perpetuate a sense of wounded racial pride in Germany.
- The **emasculation** of Germany's armed forces (limited to an army of 100,000 men, no air force, only six capital ships, etc.) was humiliating for a country with such a strong military tradition, but easily evaded (the military inspectorate was withdrawn in 1927 as a gesture of goodwill!) and Germany remained potentially strong.

Key question
Was the peace fair?

Key date

Treaty of Versailles, just one of several treaties known collectively as the Paris Peace Settlement: 28 June 1919

Key terms

Idealism
The practice of pursuing things in a perfect way, or trying to reach a very high standard, which can be unrealistic, as some ideas can exist in the mind but not in reality.

Pragmatism
The practice of dealing with matters in a way that seems practical and realistic, instead of following any preconceived theory.

Diktat
A categorical statement or decree, especially terms imposed by a victor after a war: a dictated peace.

Principle of national self-determination
The idea that people of the same linguistic, racial and cultural background should be allowed to govern themselves within a single nation state.

Emasculation
To deprive of force, weaken.

The 'Big Three' at Versailles in 1919 (left to right): Clemenceau, Wilson and Lloyd George. They look quite pleased with themselves, but this picture is designed to portray unanimity and disguises the deep differences between them.

Conclusion

The French position, advocating the movement eastwards of the existing border between France and Germany up to the Rhine river, the creation of an independent Rhineland state separate from the rest of Germany and the League of Nations as a military alliance, made a lot of sense – and perhaps the other extreme (a soft peace that hardly penalised Germany at all) made sense too. However, the truth is that just as the Germans did not accept that they had caused the war, so too they questioned whether they had truly lost it. As has already been indicated, it was the defeat itself that the German people found so hard to accept. Thus, any peace treaty that treated Germany as the defeated party was bound to be unacceptable to the German people.

No consensus

Of course, it is true to say that a great number of the treaty clauses were flawed; putting a time limit of 15 years on the occupation of the Rhineland was storing up trouble for the future (although permanent occupation was obviously not a viable alternative either) and the creation of new states in Central and Eastern Europe led to chronic destabilisation and a power vacuum conducive to German expansion, but perhaps it was really

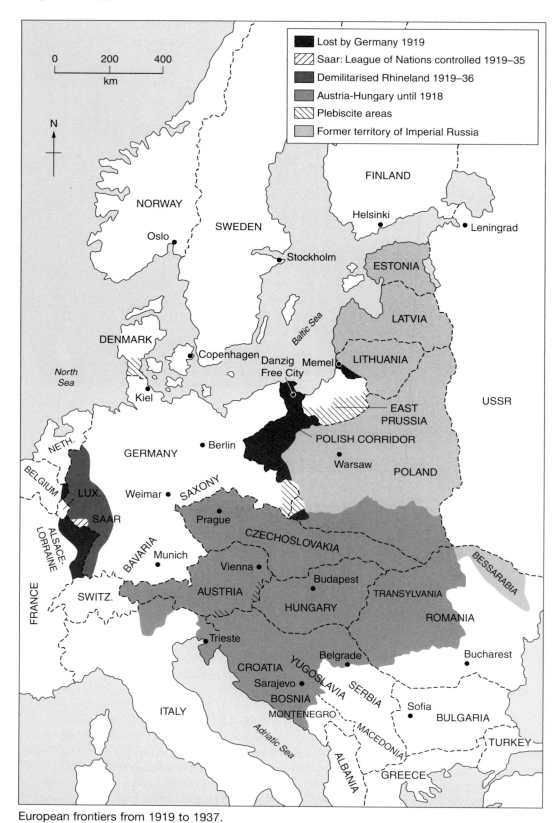

European frontiers from 1919 to 1937.

the failure to enforce the Treaty that was the nub of the problem. And the reason for this was the subsequent breakdown of consensus: all three architects of the peace treaty were soon out of office.

Wilson had a stroke later in 1919 and **Congress** refused to ratify the Treaty; Lloyd George hung on until 1922, but the British soon came to see the peace as too harsh and favoured some revision; Clemenceau fell at the beginning of 1920 and although French policy remained consistently hostile to Germany for the time being, the collapse of consensus meant that France was left very much in the lurch, with a colossal debt and little security. Germany's population of 60 million still looked pretty formidable to France's 40 million, and it is clear that, for France, Versailles failed to solve the threat posed by Germany's natural predominance in Europe. After all, Germany had not been scarred by occupation in the war and the 1914 barriers to expansion in the east were now gone.

Eastern Europe

Inevitably the peace was a compromise and it turned out to be a strange cocktail of:

- Wilsonian idealism (e.g. the League of Nations and the principle of self-determination)
- French revenge (reparations, war guilt, etc.)
- British pragmatism (temporary occupation of the Saar and Rhineland, **plebiscite** over the neutrality of Danzig, the partition of Silesia).

The real problems were created by the Treaties of St Germain (with Austria) and Trianon (with Hungary), which meant that Germany was now bordered by the relatively weak states of Austria, Poland and Czechoslovakia (see the map opposite). Of course, Poland, Czechoslovakia and Yugoslavia to the south were not created by the peace settlement, but merely recognised by it: these states had emerged towards the end of the war as the old Russian and Austrian empires broke up. Given the fact that eastern Europe and the Balkans were a bewildering kaleidoscope of races and religion, it is hardly surprising that within the new states there were minority groups who did not want to be there and who looked to a neighbouring state for protection. The opportunities for a sufficiently powerful state to disrupt the new order were obvious.

Gone was the stabilising influence of the (Austrian) Habsburg Empire, which had somehow kept these ethnic tensions in balance, and gone too was Tsarist Russia. In the east there now lurked the **Soviet Union**, initially weak, but with a new form of government that threatened to undermine the established order. It was the aim of the Soviet government to bring about world revolution and replace **capitalism** with **communism**. And it should also be remembered that Germany was not the only dissatisfied power: Hungary, the above-mentioned Soviet Union and even Italy were not happy with the outcome. The Paris Peace

Key terms

Congress
The US parliament consisting of an upper house (the Senate) and a lower house (the House of Representatives).

Plebiscite
The direct vote of all the electors of a state.

Soviet Union
The Communist state that emerged from the Russian Empire after the revolution of 1917. The full title was the Union of Soviet Socialist Republics – the USSR for short.

Capitalism
An economic system in which the production and distribution of goods depends on invested private capital and profit-making.

Communism
A political theory derived from Marxism advocating a society in which all property is publicly owned and each person is paid and works according to his or her needs and abilities.

Settlement created as many problems as it solved. Yet, as has already been stated, it was the failure to enforce the peace terms that really undermined the settlement.

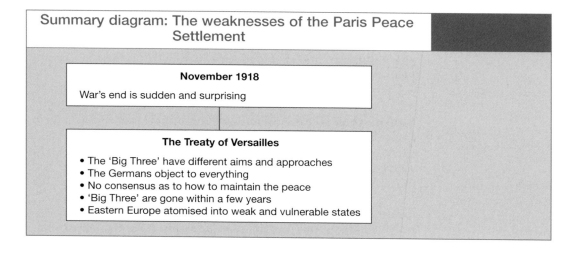

Summary diagram: The weaknesses of the Paris Peace Settlement

November 1918

War's end is sudden and surprising

The Treaty of Versailles

- The 'Big Three' have different aims and approaches
- The Germans object to everything
- No consensus as to how to maintain the peace
- 'Big Three' are gone within a few years
- Eastern Europe atomised into weak and vulnerable states

4 | Keeping the Peace

A new world

First of all it is important to remember that the First World War was the most destructive war there had ever been. Thus, regardless of the specific terms of the peace settlement, the war had in many ways created a new, unstable world in which economies had been distorted and traditional ruling systems swept away. It had also had a considerable psychological impact. The new situation was fluid, the potential for danger considerable. In these circumstances any peace settlement might fail and there was no shortage of **Jeremiahs** who were prepared to say as much.

Marshal Foch, the French commander of the Allied armies, condemned the Versailles settlement as 'an **armistice** for 20 years'. This proved to be remarkably prescient, but we should remember that the Second World War was not inevitable from this point. After all, either the peace had to be enforced or, failing that, there had to be a revision of its terms and some form of reconciliation. But to achieve either of these there had to be a common approach by the powers. Unfortunately consensus and co-operation were the first casualties in the post-war period.

Consensus evaporates

The successful implementation of the peace very much depended on the involvement of the USA. However, US failure to **ratify** the treaties and withdrawal into, if not isolation, then indifference, unhinged the settlement from the very start. No doubt, had Britain and France been able to agree on a common policy, the settlement of 1919 might have served as a basis for a lasting

Key question
Why were the terms of the peace not enforced?

Key terms

Jeremiahs
Doleful or pessimistic people; dismal prophets (from a biblical figure).

Armistice
An agreement to stop fighting temporarily.

Ratify
To confirm an agreement formally, to give it validity.

Key question
Why did 'Big Three' co-operation end?

Treaty of Rapallo:
16 April 1922

Ruhr occupation:
11 January 1923–
27 August 1925

Dawes Plan:
9 April 1924

Hyperinflation
Excessive price
increases and a
corresponding fall
in the value of
money. In the case
of Germany in 1923
the government
printed large
amounts of
banknotes which
very rapidly became
worthless.

Dawes Plan
Revised reparation
payment plan
drawn up by
Charles Dawes, the
US Vice-President
in 1924.

Reparation
Compensation for
war damage.

Bilateral
Affecting or
between two parties.

peace, but unfortunately they could not. Britain was
preoccupied with its imperial commitments and soon favoured a
revision of the peace, while France alone favoured its rigid
implementation. In truth of course both these powers had been
seriously weakened by the war and had come to depend on the
USA. They were not strong enough to enforce the peace in all its
aspects.

French occupation of the Ruhr 1923

From the very beginning, the Germans were disinclined to
comply with the treaty terms and in 1922 actually made a covert
deal with the Russians at Rapallo to disguise rearmament
(economic co-operation was a cover for military co-operation). At
the end of that year another default on reparation payments led
to a French and Belgian occupation of the Ruhr in January 1923.
This had the most serious consequences, not just for Germany,
where **hyperinflation** wreaked havoc on the middle class, but for
France, which found itself isolated. In this sense, the Ruhr
occupation was very much a defeat for the French.

The crisis was eventually resolved by the USA, which by the
Dawes Plan rescheduled German payments and obtained loans
for it. This clearly undermined Versailles and French policy, and
was a settlement favourable to Germany. Indeed, it was the US
insistence on debt repayment (the USA had loaned the Western
democracies a great deal of money during the course of the war)
that made **reparation** payments so vital for France and poisoned
European relations throughout the 1920s.

The French dilemma

In 1919 France had been led to believe it would receive Anglo-
American military guarantees to protect itself against any future
German aggression. However, these did not materialise once the
US Congress rejected the treaties. Hence, France made a number
of **bilateral** agreements, with Poland in 1921 and with
Czechoslovakia in 1924, but these offered little security; some
might say the contrary as France was committed to their
protection. From 1920 to 1925 France tried and failed to obtain a
military alliance with Britain. In the absence of an agreement,
French leaders would not contemplate any revision of the peace
settlement or any form of disarmament. They also tried to beef
up the League of Nations, but again Britain would not co-
operate. Britain could not afford European military commitments
when it had so many imperial ones; and, in any event, now that
Germany no longer had a navy or an empire, it was no longer
seen as a major threat.

Locarno Treaty 1925

In 1925 the Germans offered a treaty to guarantee the western frontiers as laid down by the Versailles Treaty. Britain and France took up this opportunity and in December 1925 signed the Locarno Treaty with Germany. At the time the Treaty was hailed as a diplomatic triumph, and the following year Germany joined the League of Nations, an act of symbolic reconciliation. However, the powers perceived the Treaty in different ways:

- for France it seemed to represent Germany's reconciliation to Versailles and a firm commitment from Britain
- for Britain it was the limit of its commitment
- for Germany it was the beginning of the revision of Versailles.

Moreover, it was significant that similar guarantees were not made for the frontiers of eastern Europe; Locarno in effect wrote off Versailles in that part of the world. Once again this was a treaty that favoured Germany.

Under the pressures created by Dawes and Locarno, French policy went on the defensive (the Maginot Line – a line of defensive fortifications along the Franco-German border – was approved in 1925, though not begun until 1929, see page 93) and was transformed from one of coercion to one of exaggerated *détente*. However, as the historian Antony Lentin wrote in 1985: 'instead of reconciling Germany to Versailles … *détente* increased German impatience and accelerated demands for further revision.' Indeed Stresemann, who is often misleadingly described as the moderate statesman of the Weimar era, wanted Allied evacuation of the Rhineland, the return of Eupen-Malmédy, of the **Saarland**, of the colonies, the annexation of Austria and even the return of **Alsace-Lorraine** (although much of this was kept secret).

Conclusion

The Locarno honeymoon (and US loans) only served to mask potential diplomatic instability and continuing German dissatisfaction. Successive German governments in the 1920s made it clear that they did not accept the eastern territorial settlement as permanent; successive German governments clandestinely rearmed (Rapallo was renewed with the Soviets in Berlin in 1926); and successive German governments continued to bleat about reparations, to such an extent that repayments were considerably scaled down by another plan, the **Young Plan** in 1929. At this time the Allies also agreed to evacuate the Rhineland the following year. When the **Great Depression** struck later in October 1929 and ended this short period of co-operation, differences about how to apply or revise the peace remained unresolved.

For Locarno to have worked it had to be accompanied by a series of negotiated concessions to Germany. French disinclination to make revisions was well known; however, between 1924 and 1929 British foreign policy under Austen Chamberlain

Key question
Was the 'Locarno honeymoon' a genuine reconciliation?

Key dates

Treaty of Locarno:
1 December 1925

Germany joined the League of Nations:
10 September 1926

Key terms

Détente
An easing of strained relations, reconciliation.

Saarland
This area, rich in mineral resources, particularly coal, was taken from Germany and administered by the League of Nations for 15 years after the Treaty of Versailles, prior to a plebiscite.

Alsace-Lorraine
French territory annexed by Germany in 1871.

Young Plan
A revised repayment schedule published in 1929 which reduced Germany's reparations burden from £6.6 billion to £2 billion.

Great Depression
The severe economic depression of 1929–34 that most historians suggest began with the Wall Street Crash.

Key dates

Young Plan: 7 June 1929

Wall Street Crash: 29 October 1929

Key term

Wall Street Crash
The collapse of prices on the New York Stock Exchange in October 1929.

also became markedly less sympathetic to the German position. As the historian Ruth Henig writes: 'The failure of the architects of the 1919 peace settlement to complete their work on an agreed basis in the decade after 1919 was one of the major factors contributing to the outbreak of war [in 1939].' However, we must not be tempted to read history backwards. Were the hopes of Locarno illusory? We will never know. The **Wall Street Crash** and world depression cut off all hopes of recovery. And it was the depression that brought Hitler to power.

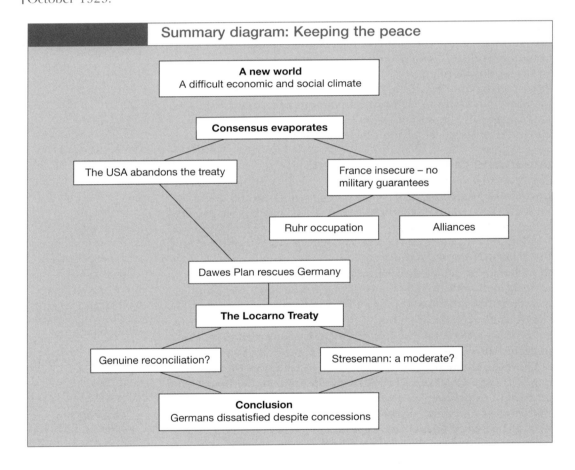

Summary diagram: Keeping the peace

A new world
A difficult economic and social climate

Consensus evaporates

The USA abandons the treaty

France insecure – no military guarantees

Ruhr occupation

Alliances

Dawes Plan rescues Germany

The Locarno Treaty

Genuine reconciliation?

Stresemann: a moderate?

Conclusion
Germans dissatisfied despite concessions

Key question
What effect did the Great Depression have on an already unstable international system?

5 | Economic Collapse and Diplomatic Instability

The Great Depression

Whatever its causes, the Great Depression that began in 1929 led to the collapse of international trade, a crisis in credit and banking and large-scale unemployment. All countries were forced to try to protect their own interests, often by means of **protective tariffs** and this, in turn, caused growing friction, an economic free-for-all and a search for self-sufficiency. The economic recovery in Europe had been excessively dependent on US loans, which operated in a triangular fashion. Basically, Germany borrowed from the USA to help pay reparations to Britain, France and Italy, and they in turn paid the money back to the USA to service war debts. With the collapse of US credit and the calling in of short-term loans, this cycle was broken.

Germany was particularly hard hit as it had borrowed more than it had ever paid in reparations, and many of its loans were short term. By May 1932, German unemployment had reached in excess of six million (30 per cent of the workforce), and this fed feelings of frustrated **nationalism**. With regard to the revision of Versailles, the German people increasingly suggested that what could not be obtained by negotiation should be demanded as a matter of right. In this atmosphere a large proportion of the German middle class, fearing another 1923 (the year of hyperinflation and ruin for many) and fearing Communist revolution, turned to the Nazi Party. Arguably the advent to power of Hitler was the most far-reaching consequence of the Depression.

Japan and the League of Nations

Another consequence of the Great Depression was the Japanese invasion of Manchuria in 1931, a part of China the Japanese had long coveted – and an area which had seen considerable Japanese investment. The invasion itself was contrived – Japan invented a Chinese terror attack on the Manchurian railway – but it led to full-scale occupation and the setting up of a puppet state – Manchukuo under the last Chinese emperor, Pui-Yi. Although militant nationalism had been growing in the Japanese Empire for some time, the loss of jobs and the collapse in rice and silk prices reinforced the position of the **right-wing military faction** – indeed the army took the initiative here without regard for the government.

However, the real significance of the invasion was that it fully exposed the weaknesses of the League of Nations. Without Soviet and US participation, and without an army of its own, the League had always been weak, although it had been able to resolve disputes between minor powers. The League was in effect controlled by Britain and France, but they often steered it in different directions. In many ways the weaknesses of the League were a reflection of the weaknesses of the democracies. Britain and France were not prepared to do anything against Japan, so when the League condemned the Japanese, Japan simply ignored the League altogether and walked out. This hardly inspired confidence for the future and was not an auspicious context for the **Disarmament Conference**, a legacy of the *détente* years, which opened in 1932. French refusal to disarm was an opportunity for Germany to demand the right to rearm (see page 28).

(see page 28)

Key terms

Protective tariffs
Taxes placed on imported goods to protect native produce.

Nationalism
Patriotic feeling, which can take an extreme form.

Right-wing military faction
A group of ultra-conservative army officers.

Disarmament Conference
The Disarmament Commission had been set up under the auspices of the League of Nations (indeed it had been one of Wilson's 14 Points) to bring about general disarmament, or at least a reduction in armaments. However, it did not meet until 1932 and was short lived.

Key dates

Japan invaded Manchuria: 18 September 1931

Disarmament Conference: February 1932

Japan left the League of Nations: March 1933

Key dates

Germany joined the League of Nations: 10 September 1926

Rearmament no longer subject to scrutiny: 31 January 1927

Rhineland evacuated: 30 June 1930

Reparations effectively abolished: 9 July 1932

Hitler became Chancellor: 30 January 1933

Germany

By 1933 Germany had in fact secured a substantial revision of the Treaty of Versailles: it was a member of the League of Nations, rearmament was no longer subject to scrutiny, the Rhineland had been evacuated and finally reparations had been in effect cancelled (at Lausanne in 1932), but it had not been achieved in a wholly satisfactory way:

- Germany continued to resent those parts of the Treaty that remained.
- France was apprehensive about the possibility of further revision in the future.
- Britain was irritated by the fact that continuing concessions had not engendered a sense of gratitude in Germany.

This was the context in which Hitler came to power in 1933.

Conclusion

The Great Depression itself clearly did not lead directly to war – war came after recovery was well under way – but its effects were far-reaching. It destroyed the positive and encouraging economic and political developments of the years between 1924 and 1930. Franco-German co-operation and the 'spirit of Locarno' fizzled out. Indeed by 1933 the hopes engendered by Locarno seemed a distant dream. Thus, the background to our main period of focus is:

- a flawed peace settlement
- no agreed means of its enforcement
- an unstable international system
- a major economic crisis.

It was therefore a time of great uncertainty for everyone, and an opportunity for an ex-corporal from Austria who had a very clear vision about how he wished the future to unfold.

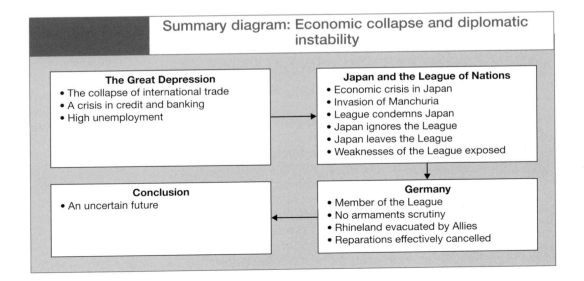

Summary diagram: Economic collapse and diplomatic instability

The Great Depression
- The collapse of international trade
- A crisis in credit and banking
- High unemployment

Japan and the League of Nations
- Economic crisis in Japan
- Invasion of Manchuria
- League condemns Japan
- Japan ignores the League
- Japan leaves the League
- Weaknesses of the League exposed

Conclusion
- An uncertain future

Germany
- Member of the League
- No armaments scrutiny
- Rhineland evacuated by Allies
- Reparations effectively cancelled

2 Hitler Challenges the Versailles Settlement 1933–6

POINTS TO CONSIDER

This chapter will look at the origins of Hitler's thinking before going on to look at his first 4 years in office, culminating in the remilitarisation of the Rhineland and the Four-Year Plan. You may wish to consider just how cautious or bold he was and how his underlying ideological position affected his behaviour in this early period (if it did at all). You should also consider to what extent Hitler had successfully thrown off the restrictions of the Versailles Treaty by 1936 and how far his success was the result of his boldness and skill or the result of the weaknesses of others.

The key areas examined are:

- Hitler's ideology
- Hitler's first 2 years in office, January 1933– January 1935
- Rearmament and reactions
- The remilitarisation of the Rhineland 1936
- The Four-Year Plan
- Conclusion 1933–6

Key dates

1920	February	Hitler and Drexler drew up the Nazi Party 25-Point Programme
1924		Hitler wrote *Mein Kampf*
1933	January 30	Hitler became Chancellor
	October 14	Hitler pulled out of both the Disarmament Conference and the League of Nations; Rapallo terminated
1934	January 26	German Non-Aggression Pact with Poland
	May 29	Disarmament Conference ended
	June 14–15	Hitler visited Mussolini
	July	Mussolini ordered troops to Austrian border to thwart Nazi coup
1935	January 13	Saar plebiscite victory for Hitler
	March 16	Hitler announced the existence of the *Luftwaffe* and the reintroduction of conscription

	April 11–14	Stresa meeting (Stresa Front)
	May 2	Franco-Soviet Mutual Assistance Pact
	June 18	Anglo-German Naval Pact
	October 3	Mussolini invaded Abyssinia
1936	March 7	Hitler moved troops into Rhineland
	July 18	Outbreak of Spanish Civil War
	October 19	Four-Year Plan formally launched
	November 1	Rome–Berlin Axis
	November 24	Anti-Comintern Pact

1 | Hitler's Ideology

Early years

Key question
What were the origins of Hitler's ideas?

Many historians contend that Hitler's belief that the Germans were a master race destined to colonise the east was fundamental to his foreign-policy thinking. If you too decide that his policy was ideology driven – that is to say, it was governed by a body of firmly held ideas and long-term plans rather than being an improvisation based on opportunities – then the origins of his thinking are of paramount importance. However, attempts to explain them by reference to his early childhood are just speculation.

It is likely that Hitler's experience from 1907 to 1913 in Vienna, where Jewish families were economically, socially and academically successful, did have an impact on his thinking and generated a feeling of **anti-Semitism**. In particular, Jewish entrants were disproportionately successful at the Academy of Fine Arts, where Hitler failed to get in. Hitler's boyhood friend from 1904 to 1908, August Kubizek, records that the young Adolf constantly complained about the multi-ethnicity of German Vienna and in particular expressed his dislike for the Jews.

Intellectual background

Racism and anti-Semitism were not unusual at that time. Anti-Semitism had a long history (going back to Jesus's death sentence requested by the **Sanhedrin**) and was particularly virulent in Austria and Germany. Indeed, specifically anti-Semitic political candidates were elected to the German *Reichstag*, admittedly in small numbers, from the 1880s. Kaiser Wilhelm II himself told Sir Edward Grey, the British Foreign Secretary, in 1907 that 'they want stamping out' and later he was to suggest gas as a means of efficient extermination.

Towards the end of the nineteenth century racism in general was given a **pseudo-scientific** boost by **social Darwinism**, the application of biological evolution to human society. Thus, Jews were not only defined in terms of religion or appearance, but in terms of a biologically determined inferior race. Human life, like animal life, was described as a struggle for survival, the 'survival of the fittest' as the philosopher Herbert Spencer put it, and the

Key terms

Anti-Semitism
Hostility or prejudice against Jews.

Sanhedrin
Highest Jewish council in ancient Jerusalem.

Pseudo-scientific
Falsely considered to be scientific.

Social Darwinism
The theory that ethnic groups are subject to the same Darwinian laws of natural selection as are plants and animals.

idea of white superiority, the superiority of the so-called (and rarely defined) Aryan race, was further developed by another British philosopher, Houston Stewart Chamberlain, whom Hitler met and admired.

These views gained wide currency. Indeed in 1914, many in the upper echelons of the German government saw the forthcoming war as a biological racial war, a struggle between **teuton** and **slav**, and even in the 1919 peace settlement Britain and the USA refused Japan's request to include a declaration of racial equality. What we have to remember, then, is that Hitler's thought was not unusual; he was very much a product of his own times, but at the same time we have to acknowledge that he later carried these ideas to unimaginably violent extremes.

The impact of the First World War on Hitler

The impact of the 1914–18 war on Hitler was no doubt considerable, but, of course, it was the shock of defeat and the desire for revenge that turned him into a political animal, as he himself stated in his autobiography. Without the defeat or indeed perhaps without such a (perceived) harsh peace settlement, it is unlikely that Hitler's views would have ever developed or been important. Of perhaps equal significance was the year after the war when Hitler attended a number of **army indoctrination courses** and discovered his considerable ability to speak to an audience.

Indeed, it is not until the post-war period that we can have any concrete evidence of Hitler's thinking. Thus, it is from 1919 onwards that we are able to build up a real picture of his thought and its later implications for foreign policy.

Sources

What are our sources up to 1933? Principally we rely on the Nazi Party **25-Point Programme** that Hitler drew up with Anton Drexler in February 1920, his semi-autobiographical book *Mein Kampf*, which was published in two volumes in 1925 and 1927, Hitler's *Second* or *Secret Book*, written in 1928, but not published until 1961, and his letters and his speeches, which date from 1919.

It is possible to identify the evolution of Hitler's thought between the years 1919 and 1924. In 1919 his foreign policy objectives were quite conventional, similar to those of the Pan-German League. In his speech of September 1919 he spoke of a 'Greater Germany'; in December 1919 he stated, 'the removal of our colonies represents an irreparable loss for us'; and in the 25-Point Programme of February 1920, it was stated:

1. We demand the union of all Germans in a Greater Germany on the basis of the right of national self-determination.
2. We demand equality of rights for the German people in its dealings with other nations, and the revocation of the peace treaties of Versailles and St. Germain.
3. We demand land and territory [colonies] to feed our people and to settle our surplus population.

Key terms

Teuton
Ancient northern European tribe, i.e. German.

Slav
Member of a group of peoples in central and eastern Europe.

Army indoctrination courses
In this context, right-wing political courses designed to train ex-soldiers to seek out and expose socialist activity.

25-Point Programme
This was the Nazi Party's first manifesto and contained a series of aims.

Key question
How do we know about Hitler's ideology?

Key date
Nazi Party 25-Point Programme: February 1920

4. Only members of the nation may be citizens of the State. Only those of German blood, whatever their creed, may be members of the nation. Accordingly no Jew may be a member of the nation.

The evolution of Hitler's thought

Key terms

Bolsheviks
Members of the Russian Communist Party; the rulers of the Soviet Union.

Blockade
The surrounding or blocking of a place, especially a port, by an enemy to prevent entry and exit of supplies, etc.

Key date

Hitler wrote *Mein Kampf*: 1924

Key question
What is the message of *Mein Kampf*?

Thus, Hitler wanted a revision of the Treaty of Versailles, the creation of a new Greater Germany to accommodate all 'pure' Germans including those Germans of the former Habsburg Empire – in Austria and Czechoslovakia – who had never been part of Germany, and the return of Germany's lost colonies. At this stage he saw France and Britain as the main obstacles and Italy as a potential ally. Russia was seen as a potential ally until he was convinced that all **Bolsheviks** were Jews. Anti-Bolshevism thus became as an important preoccupation to Hitler as anti-Semitism.

The French occupation of the Ruhr in 1923 changed his perspective somewhat, as Britain opposed the operation, and he came to see it as a potential ally too. He actually admired the British, not only for their Empire, but because he also felt that there was a racial affinity. However, an alliance with Britain would preclude the recovery of the colonies, and thus Hitler came to think in terms of acquiring territory elsewhere, in the east. Accordingly, by the time he wrote *Mein Kampf* he had further developed points 3 and 4 of the Nazi programme.

Mein Kampf

Hitler was convinced that the outcome of the great racial struggle would depend on population, territory and resources, but Germany was 'a nation without space' (the **blockade** had demonstrated its vulnerability). The only solution was the acquisition of living space (*lebensraum*) in the east (which to some extent echoed what happened at the Treaty of Brest-Litovsk in March 1918, see page 3). This could only be achieved by struggle; Hitler rejected peaceful economic means to achieve these aims. As he stuck religiously to this policy and it had important implications for later foreign policy, it is worth quoting *Mein Kampf* at length:

Germany has an annual increase in population of nearly 900,000. The difficulty of feeding this army of new citizens must increase from year to year and ultimately end in catastrophe unless ways and means are found … Nature knows no boundaries … she confers the master's right on her favourite child, the strongest in courage and industry. … Only a sufficiently large space on this earth can ensure the independent existence of a nation. … As members of the highest species of humanity on this earth, we have a[n] obligation … [to] … fulfil. … The acquisition of land and soil [must be] the objective of our foreign policy. … The demand for the restoration of the frontiers of 1914 is a political absurdity. … We are … turning our eyes towards the land in the East. … The colossal empire in the east is ripe for dissolution. And the end of the Jewish domination in Russia will also be the end of Russia as a state. ... Today we are not struggling to achieve a position as a world power; we must fight for the existence of our fatherland, for the unity of our nation and the daily bread of our children. If we look around for allies from this point of view, only two states remain: England and Italy.

Profile: Adolf Hitler 1889–1945

1889	–	Born in Braunau in Austria on 20 April
1907	–	Went to Vienna to become an artist, but was unsuccessful and became a drifter
1913	–	Went to Munich and joined the German army in 1914, served in the war, and was awarded the Iron Cross First Class
1919	–	Joined the Nazi party and became its leader
1923–4	–	Imprisoned for 9 months after the failure of an attempted coup (the Munich *Putsch*). In prison he wrote his semi-autobiographical work *Mein Kampf* ('My Struggle') in which he expounded his views on race and space
1930, 1932	–	The Depression brought the Nazis dramatic success in elections
1933	–	Became Chancellor on 30 January
1936	–	Remilitarised the Rhineland
1938	–	*Anschluss* with Austria, and the annexation of part of Czechoslovakia
1939	–	Germany attacked on Poland, leading to the outbreak of the Second World War in September
1940	–	Defeated France (but not Britain)
1941	–	Invaded Russia (Operation Barbarossa)
1943	–	Failure of the Barbarossa campaign
1944	–	Western front opened up
1945	–	Committed suicide with his wife, Eva Braun, in his bunker in Berlin on 30 April

In many ways Hitler's rise to power was quite remarkable. A loner and a failed artist, he did not discover his talent for oratory until he was in his thirties, but even so his track record as a politician in the 1920s was one of failure. It was not until the Great Depression struck in 1929 that the 'Bohemian Corporal' (he was born Austrian and never rose above the rank of corporal) became a popular figure. Hitler's twin obsessions were race and space. He was determined to overthrow Versailles, unite all Germans and conquer 'living space' in the east. This could only be achieved by war, which Hitler considered a noble endeavour; however, it is likely that he would have preferred to have conducted a series of short, sharp campaigns, rather than the great conflagration he precipitated. As far as the Jews were concerned, he considered them vermin and their extermination was the logical consequence of his appalling racial theories.

Four and a Half Years Struggle against Lies, Stupidity and Cowardice. A Reckoning by Adolf Hitler. The front cover of *Mein Kampf* published in 1925.

Hitler (left) in prison in the Landsberg fortress in 1924. Clearly living conditions and visiting rights were surprisingly good.

The *Second* or *Secret Book*

The *Second* or *Secret Book*, written just a few years later, was largely a restatement of *Mein Kampf*, although Hitler did express concern about France's alliances with Poland (1921) and Czechoslovakia (1924), which seemed to hem Germany in, and he did address Britain's policy of trying to keep a balance of power on the continent by ensuring that no single power came to dominate. This balance of power policy he believed to be incorrect, as a Greater Germany was no threat to the world-wide interests of the British Empire. However, he did point out there was no limit to the expansion of a racially superior nation.

Key question
How did the *Secret Book* differ from *Mein Kampf*?

Race and space

It cannot be emphasised too often that race and space remained central to Hitler's thinking throughout:

- the union of all Germans, the master race, in a Greater Germany and
- *lebensraum* in the east.

Hitler was obsessive about these fundamental concepts. He held them with a messianic fervour. How far this was a novel policy is a moot point. Expansionism had been fundamental to the 'men of 1914' in the September Programme (see page 3), and in the Treaty of Brest-Litovsk; they also saw warfare as a biological struggle between the races, between teuton and slav. However, Hitler brought these two concepts together with greater intensity and carried them to their logical and appalling conclusion.

Speeches and testament

Hitler returned to the same theme in speech after speech between 1928 and 1933, but naturally, when he came into office in 1933, he stopped making reference to these ideas in public. Yet in private, as we shall see, he constantly returned to them – in briefings, in letters, in his **Table Talk** during the war and finally in his **Political Testament**. Indeed, the consistency of Hitler's views both before and after coming to power is really quite striking. It appears his views became fixed at an early stage and never really altered.

Of course, not all historians subscribe to the primacy of ideology as the most important element in Hitler's foreign policy. Some see him as more of an opportunist and point out the contradictions in his actions, but we will consider this alternative view later (see page 82). For the time being it is essential that you at least keep the question in the back of your mind – was Hitler's foreign policy ideology driven? If you accept that it was, then it is clear that German expansion meant war. However, dreams of conquest and empire are one thing, reality is another. How was Hitler going to achieve such fantastic objectives?

Key terms

Table Talk
A collection of stenographic notes which purport to record some of Hitler's private conversations between 1941 and 1944.

Political Testament
Hitler's last will and testament which was drawn up in the bunker in Berlin in April 1945 when the Soviets were closing in.

Summary diagram: Hitler's ideology

Origins
- Early years in Vienna
- Intellectual context
- War and defeat

Sources
- *Mein Kampf*
- *Secret* or *Second Book*
- Later speeches and private conversations

Race and space
- Some of Hitler's views were not unusual …
- … but he carried them to violent extremes
- Hitler's views seem to have been quite consistent: they did not change

---

Key question
What did Hitler achieve in his first year in office?

Key date
Hitler became Chancellor: 30 January 1933

Key terms

Coalition
Temporary alliance of political parties to form a government.

SA
Sturmabteilung, 'storm division'; the Nazi Party's paramilitary force founded in 1921.

Führer
The German word for leader.

2 | Hitler's First Two Years in Office, January 1933–January 1935

The first year

It is important to remember that when Hitler became Chancellor in January 1933 he did not have full control over the government (he was in a **coalition**), over the army (the soldiers owed allegiance to President Hindenburg) or even over his own party (Ernst Röhm and the **SA**, the brown-shirted Nazi stormtroopers used to enforce 'discipline', were by no means his poodles). Accordingly, he had to proceed with caution.

It would therefore be some years before he could really take the initiative with regard to international affairs. In any event, in this matter he stepped on to a moving conveyer belt, as it were, with events already in train (see Chapter 1), and although he had long-term objectives, he had no detailed plan – indeed no real idea how he was going to achieve them. However, such concerns did not in any way deflect Hitler from his long-term goals.

Dictatorial power

Throughout 1933 and 1934 (see the box on page 29) Hitler took steps to consolidate his position within Germany, assuming dictatorial powers, banning other parties, eliminating Röhm and his cronies (as much to please the army as himself) and, after the death of Hindenburg, assuming the presidency (and the title of *Führer*) to which the army owed an oath of loyalty (August 1934).

In private, Hitler continued to express his true objectives. As early as 3 February 1933 he told the generals that Versailles had

Paul von Hindenburg had risen to the rank of general prior to retirement in 1911. He was recalled in 1914 and together with General Ludendorff was able to defeat the Russian invasion of east Prussia. Although unable to repeat this success on the Western front, he remained a national hero and 'father figure', so much so that he was elected President of the Weimar Republic in 1925 and re-elected in 1932. He died in 1934. This picture is a painting of about 1916.

to be overthrown, that rearmament was the most pressing priority, that '**National Service** must be reintroduced' and that, once Germany was sufficiently powerful, the regime would achieve 'the conquest of new living space in the east and its ruthless Germanisation'.

Germany leaves the League

In public Hitler protested his desire for peace in a series of speeches and interviews throughout 1933, stating 'nobody wishes for peace more than I'. These utterances were of course designed to camouflage the Nazi consolidation of power and an acceleration in rearmament. In fact, the whole question of armaments was currently centre stage at the Disarmament Conference in Geneva (see page 18). Prior to Hitler, the foreign ministry had already taken a hard line on this issue, requesting parity of armaments; now in October 1933, using France's refusal to accept this point, Hitler pulled out of both the Conference and the League of Nations and cleverly held a **confirmatory plebiscite** in November, achieving 95 per cent approval.

Collapse of the Disarmament Conference

What helped Hitler at this time was a growing change in attitude in Britain. By the 1930s a new historical climate was emerging which suggested that Germany had not been solely responsible for the outbreak of the First World War after all: responsibility was collective. Accordingly, the British government was quite

National Service
Conscription; compulsory enlistment for military service.

Confirmatory plebiscite
A vote to approve what has been done.

Key terms

Germany left the League of Nations: 14 October 1933

Key date

Reichstag fire
The burning of the *Reichstag* in February 1933, an act which the Nazis blamed on the Communists and which enabled them to arrest and restrict opponents in the election campaign.

Enabling Act (1933)
Enabled Hitler to operate as a dictator for 4 years without recourse to Parliament (*Reichstag*).

Gestapo
Short for *Geheime Staatspolizei*: secret state police.

Non-Aggression Pact
An agreement not to go to war with each other.

TIMELINE OF HITLER'S CONSOLIDATION OF POWER

1933

January 30	Hitler became Chancellor
February 27	***Reichstag* fire**
February 28	Hitler given emergency powers
March 3	Communists arrested
March 5	Hitler won 44 per cent of the vote in the election
March 23	**Enabling Act** gave Hitler 4 years' dictatorial power
March 31	Local government brought under Nazi control
May 2	Trade unions banned
July 14	Germany officially became a one-party state
November 30	***Gestapo*** created

1934

June 30	'Night of the Long Knives' – SA purged
August 2	President Hindenburg died

Hitler combined the offices of Chancellor and President and proclaimed himself *Führer*. Army swore oath of allegiance to him.

German Non-Aggression Pact with Poland: 26 January 1934

Disarmament Conference ended: 29 May 1934

prepared to allow some German rearmament, which it knew was already secretly under way, provided it was the result of negotiation and agreement. In order to get Germany back into the conference, Britain proposed:

- an increase in the German army (to 200,000 – up from the Versailles ceiling of 100,000)
- a reduction in the French army (from 500,000 to 200,000)
- that Germany should have an air force half the size of the French.

Indeed Britain spent 6 months trying to get Germany back into the talks and this gave Hitler excellent cover for the first risky stages of rearmament. No one wished to torpedo the conference by denouncing Germany, but France finally blew the whistle in April 1934 by pointing out that the German budget was clearly designed for rearmament. This finally brought the Disarmament Conference to an end. In the meantime Hitler attempted to make bilateral agreements, starting with Britain, suggesting Germany would guarantee the British Empire in return for a free hand in Eastern Europe and proposing a **Non-Aggression Pact** and a Naval Agreement (November 1933), but Britain would not be drawn at this stage.

The second year

The Polish Pact

Much to everyone's surprise, on 26 January 1934, Hitler concluded a Non-Aggression Pact with Poland against the wishes of the German foreign ministry. Although the initiative to some extent came from Poland, Hitler had good reasons for concluding this agreement – it was designed to upset the French government (which had an alliance with Poland and was therefore an obstacle to his plans) and reflected his wish to move away from Russia.

The Rapallo Treaty, which had originally been signed between the Weimar Republic and the Soviet Union in 1922 (see page 15), had been terminated at the end of 1933 and Soviet overtures in March 1934 were rebuffed. As the Polish Pact also risked Hitler's popularity, in view of the German dislike of Polish 'occupation' of German territory (the Polish corridor cutting off East Prussia – see the map on page 12), many foreign observers regarded it as an **act of statesmanship**. Of course, we know, with hindsight, that it was merely a cynical ploy to buy time. Hitler said privately at the time, 'I have no intention of maintaining a serious friendship with Poland'.

The Austrian crisis

In June 1934 Hitler visited Mussolini to cultivate his friendship, but the meeting was not a success; *Il Duce* was not impressed. Moreover, the following month, when the Austrian Nazis assassinated Chancellor Dollfuss and attempted a coup, Mussolini ordered troops to the Austrian border to indicate his opposition to any such action. Relations with Germany became tense. Although the Austrian Nazis had probably acted on their own initiative, it should be remembered that Hitler, an Austrian by birth, was committed to *Anschluss* in the long term. This was a dangerous time for the German leader, but as we shall see (page 34) the democracies were insufficiently united to devise a co-ordinated policy with Italy against Germany. Although in September, the Soviet Union joined the League of Nations and Britain and France issued a guarantee of Austrian independence, there was no attempt to take any concrete steps against Hitler.

The Saar plebiscite

In the final months of 1934 Hitler concentrated on preparations for the plebiscite in the Saar, which was held by the League of Nations in accordance with the terms of the Treaty of Versailles. In 1919 the Saarland had been, in effect, placed under French control for 15 years and now the people were being offered the chance of returning to the Reich. The plebiscite was held in January 1935 and resulted in an overwhelming vote (90.9 per cent) in favour of return. This was a triumph for Hitler. It was a free and fair vote which the Nazis could not manipulate. It was, therefore, a genuine expression of the popular will in the Saarland.

Key question
What did Hitler achieve in his second year?

Key terms

Act of statesmanship
A skilful and mature act.

Il Duce
'The leader', as Mussolini was known.

Key dates

Hitler visited Mussolini: 14–15 June 1934

Mussolini ordered troops to the Austrian border: July 1934

Saar plebiscite victory for Hitler: 13 January 1935

Key question
Why was the Saar plebiscite such a significant boost to Hitler's prestige?

Hitler had survived a period of extreme vulnerability unscathed, and, at the end of 2 years in office, was in a much stronger position. Now he no longer felt the need to disguise his rearmament programme.

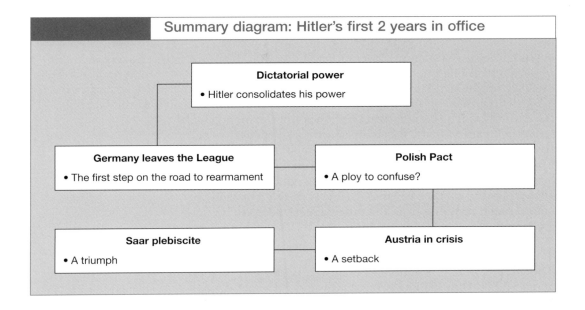

Summary diagram: Hitler's first 2 years in office

Dictatorial power
- Hitler consolidates his power

Germany leaves the League
- The first step on the road to rearmament

Polish Pact
- A ploy to confuse?

Saar plebiscite
- A triumph

Austria in crisis
- A setback

Key question
How did the Western democracies respond to Hitler's blatant defiance of the Treaty of Versailles?

Key date

Hitler announced the existence of the *Luftwaffe* and the reintroduction of conscription: 16 March 1935

3 | Rearmament and Reactions

From the very beginning, Germany had ignored the rearmament clauses of the Versailles Treaty; aircraft had been built and the army had been trained and expanded, usually with the co-operation of the Soviet Union. There was, therefore, considerable continuity between Weimar and Nazi policy (although not in terms of co-operation with the USSR). However, Hitler dramatically increased the pace. As early as the beginning of February 1933 he informed both the generals and the cabinet that rearmament was the main priority, and, of course, in this policy he had the full support of the armed forces and the old conservative élite. By 1935 it was becoming impossible to disguise the growth of the armed forces, and on 4 March Britain gave German armaments as a reason for new rearmament plans. A few days later the French extended the period of military service. Cleverly exploiting these moves by the democracies, Hitler then announced the existence of the *Luftwaffe*, and on 16 March issued a decree introducing conscription, coupled with a declaration that Germany had no further intention of observing the defence limitations of the Versailles Treaty.

Key term

Luftwaffe
Literally 'air weapon'; German for air force.

Increases in the armed forces
As early as December 1932 plans had been activated by the Weimar Republic to triple the army from 100,000 to 300,000 men. So by 1935 the army had increased from seven to 21

divisions, and conscription envisaged a further increase to 36 (over half a million men). Similarly the *Luftwaffe* grew from just a few hundred planes in 1932 to some 2500 by 1935. However, as a proportion of the gross national product (**GNP**), military expenditure was still relatively low, and it was not until 1936 that rearmament was really stepped up.

Nevertheless, expenditure had increased from 2.7 billion marks in 1933 to 8 billion marks in 1935 (see the table on page 69), enough to give Germany greater comparability with the other powers, and enough to cause them concern. Germany was now catching up. Indeed Hitler went out of his way to exaggerate the extent of rearmament (claiming in March 1935, for instance, that the *Luftwaffe* was as large as Britain's Royal Air Force), because it seems he believed that a Germany which was perceived to be strong would not be attacked – not that any of the other powers planned to do this – and he no doubt felt that such bluff might lead the other powers to make concessions. But why was Hitler allowed to tear up the Versailles Treaty so easily? The lack of any co-ordinated response from the other powers needs to be explained.

The response of the democracies

The ambassadors of Britain and France in Berlin had no illusions about Hitler. André François-Poncet warned Paris that the new Chancellor was a man of action rather than words, and in a series of reports Sir Horace Rumbold told London that Hitler was a serious threat to Germany's neighbours and the peace of the world. The French government took their man's impressions seriously, but Britain was not a neighbour and the government felt that Rumbold was alarmist. **Whitehall** felt that power would tame Hitler and make him respectable; his earlier rhetoric was not taken literally, although his desire to revise Versailles was recognised. In any event, as has been indicated earlier, with the growing belief that the responsibility for the catastrophe of 1914 should be shared among the powers, the punitive aspects of the 1919 peace settlement no longer seemed justified.

France

There are several reasons why the democracies failed to stand up to Hitler. In the case of France there was widespread revulsion against war and some sympathy for the League of Nations and the concept of disarmament. Internally there were ideological conflicts and frequent changes of government that led to paralysis in policy-making. There were three changes of government in 1932, four in 1933, two in 1934 and two in 1935. Moreover, the worst effects of the Depression struck France later than in other countries, so that by the mid-1930s the economy was extremely weak.

In addition, French foreign policy and military planning were totally incompatible. Military planning was entirely defensive, whereas foreign policy revolved around giving guarantees to the states of Eastern Europe (in an arrangement known as the '**Little Entente**'), guarantees that were impossible to fulfil without some

Key term

GNP
The total value of goods produced and services provided in a country in a year plus the total of net income from abroad in the same period.

Key question
Why did the democracies fail to stand up to Hitler?

Key terms

Whitehall
A street in London where many government offices are located; hence a name for the British government.

Little *Entente*
So-called because it was an agreement (*entente*) with a small number of minor powers – Czechoslovakia, Yugoslavia and Romania – signed in 1922.

sort of offensive capability. The French air force was ineffectual, with no bombing capacity, and army numbers were insufficient. For these reasons, France relied increasingly on Britain and was unable to take an independent line in foreign affairs. France would have liked to take a tougher line against Germany, but it was just not possible, because Britain would not do so (for a fuller discussion of French and British policy, see Chapter 5).

Britain

Support for disarmament, the League of Nations and pacifism was widespread in Britain too. But Britain remained primarily a maritime and imperial power. Its eyes were not fixed on the European continent, and this is where Britain and France diverged. Britain avoided fixed commitments and would not tie itself to France. Its concern was principally the defence of the Empire, and its army was widely dispersed to fulfil imperial tasks. Britain had global commitments and too few resources. It had to keep an eye on not only Europe, but the Mediterranean and, in particular, the Far East as well, where Japan was active.

Simultaneous defence of all these areas was beyond Britain's capability; moreover, defence expenditure was not something that could be dramatically increased without compromising people's living standards, which were only just recovering from the Depression. This, in turn, would obviously have had significant political consequences: in short, possible electoral defeat for the politicians who carried out such a policy. These latter points applied to France as well.

However, where Britain and France diverged quite significantly was over Germany. The British attitude was that the Versailles Treaty had been unfair to Germany and needed revision. This, of course, played into Hitler's hands. But Britain still considered itself to be a great power, a moral leader in the world, and as such felt that it had a right, a responsibility and indeed legitimate interests which entitled it to be involved in any revision. In British eyes changes had to be managed by consensus rather than made **unilaterally**.

Accordingly, there was a feeling that Hitler should be, and could be, accommodated, that it would be possible to do business with him. Furthermore, he was not considered a threat at this stage and, compared with Soviet communism, was seen as very much the lesser evil.

Concerns about Germany

Britain and France worked hard to make the Disarmament Conference (1932–4) work. Hitler's withdrawal from both the Conference and the League presented the democracies with a dilemma. As we have already seen, France favoured a tough line but Britain did not. Anglo-French relations were not good at this time. However, by 1935 there was a growing realisation that something had to be done about Hitler. In February Britain and France pieced together a new plan that involved Germany's return to the League, a reciprocal agreement against air attack

Key term

Unilaterally
Done by or affecting one person or group or country, etc. and not another.

and the legitimisation of German rearmament. At the same time (as has already been noted), Britain announced new defence preparations in March. But it was the matter of the Nazi threat to Austrian independence made manifest by the assassination of Dollfuss in July 1934 that drew Britain, France and Italy together.

The 'Stresa Front'

France and Italy had already signed the Rome Agreements in January 1935 which settled some African questions. Between 11 and 14 April Ramsay MacDonald, the British Prime Minister, and Sir John Simon, the Foreign Secretary, met with Pierre Laval, the French Foreign Minister, and Benito Mussolini, the Italian dictator, at Stresa to discuss German rearmament and the status of Austria. This led to a strongly worded condemnation of Germany's actions and reaffirmed the commitment to Locarno (see page 16) and Austrian independence. Britain also induced the League in Geneva to condemn Germany.

The so-called 'Stresa Front' offered some hope for peace and could have thwarted Hitler; Sir Eric Phipps, British ambassador to Germany (Rumbold's successor), reported that 'Stresa made Hitler scratch his head, Geneva made him lose it', suggesting that the German leader might have been unnerved by these developments. However, he issued a secret **Defence Law** very soon afterwards, on 21 May, so he does not appear to have been deterred at all. In any event, the so-called Stresa Front proved to be only a 9-day wonder and evidence of the disunity of the Western powers was not long delayed. On 2 May 1935 France and Russia concluded a treaty of mutual assistance, which did not meet with much approval in either Rome or London.

The Anglo-German Naval Pact

Hitler promptly took advantage of British displeasure to launch a fresh initiative (although not an original proposal) on 21 May. This quickly led on 18 June to the Anglo-German Naval Pact, which restricted the German navy to 35 per cent of British strength. This undermined the Versailles Treaty and the Stresa Front and dealt a considerable blow to Anglo-French co-operation since there had been no consultation with the French government. This was a good deal for Hitler because the German navy had nothing like 35 per cent of British capacity and it therefore allowed him, in theory, to triple existing levels. Once again, German rearmament was given official sanction. Hitler was understandably delighted with the agreement.

From the British point of view it seemed sensible to take advantage of the offer of a voluntary agreement – particularly since Japan had withdrawn from the **Washington and London naval treaties** the previous December. It also seemed to rule out another naval race, like the one before the First World War. Anything that took pressure off the Royal Navy was to be welcomed at this time.

Stresa meeting: 11–14 April 1935

Franco-Soviet Mutual Assistance Pact: 2 May 1935

Anglo-German Naval Pact: 18 June 1935

Defence Law
By this law Dr Schacht, the Minister of Finance, was given authority to 'direct the economic preparations for war'.

Washington and London naval treaties
The Washington naval agreement was signed in 1922 by Britain, the USA, Japan and others to restrict the size of navies.

Key date

Mussolini invaded Abyssinia: 3 October 1935

The dictators emboldened

So the democracies were once again out of step even before the Abyssinian episode – Mussolini's unpopular invasion of the African state in October (see page 52) – dealt the death-blow to any attempt to present a united front to Hitler. Thereafter the initiative passed to the dictators.

What enabled Hitler to pursue his aims with greater confidence and flexibility was the diplomatic revolution that occurred in these years. The main cause of this change was the Italian dictator, Benito Mussolini – 'the man who took the lid off' in Low's cartoon – whose actions over Abyssinia (today Ethiopia) led to a split with the democracies and reconciliation with Germany (see Chapter 3).

Benito Mussolini: the man who took the lid off. A David Low cartoon published in the London *Evening Standard* in 1935.

Summary diagram: Rearmament and reactions

Conscription

- Hitler increases the size of the army
- Hitler announces the existence of the air force
- Hitler declares that the military clauses of Versailles are no more

Response

- France weak; depends on Britain
- Britain also vulnerable, but feels Versailles can be improved by negotiation
- Stresa Front: Britain, France and Italy condemn Germany, but ...
- ... Anglo-German Naval Pact completely undermines the Stresa Front

4 | The Remilitarisation of the Rhineland 1936

The occupation

Now that the Allies were preoccupied with Italy's invasion of Abyssinia, Hitler decided to move into the Rhineland despite the nervousness of both the army and the foreign ministry. In a conversation with his ambassador in Rome, Ulrich von Hassell, in February 1936, Hitler said he originally intended to postpone this step until the spring of 1937, but despite the fact that 'militarily Germany was not yet ready' Hitler felt the time was right. He was prepared to gamble and he used the ratification of the Franco-Soviet Pact at the end of February (it had initially been signed in May 1935) as a pretext, claiming that it was incompatible with the Locarno Treaty. On 2 March Hitler issued the order and 5 days later he moved troops into the Rhineland – on a Saturday to avoid any immediate response.

At the same time Hitler offered negotiations on new demilitarised zones on both sides of the border, non-aggression pacts with France and Belgium, and mutual guarantees against attacks from the air. As the historian William Craig writing in 1978 observed: 'The mixture of [a] military *fait accompli* with [a] diplomatic smokescreen was masterly, and the temptation for nervous and peace-loving governments to examine the offer was overwhelming.' This offer in itself was enough to disarm the British government. Since the (premature) allied evacuation of the area in 1930 it had been the intention of all German governments to remilitarise the Rhineland (see the map on page 12), and Britain and France had been expecting negotiations for some time. However, despite all the warnings, the French government neither challenged German intentions nor saw to it that its armed forces were ready to resist.

Winston Churchill later wrote that if the French had taken military action immediately, Britain would have been forced to lend France support. Many people came to assume that this was an opportunity missed. Hitler could have been stopped here in 1936 and even brought down – a view reinforced by Hitler's later remarks that if the German troops had been attacked, they had orders to retreat. But is this contention that Hitler could have been stopped true?

The reaction

The German forces were undoubtedly small: we cannot be precise, but about 30,000 including a substantial proportion of armed police seems the best guess. However, their instructions were to resist if challenged and make a fighting retreat. Behind them stood the entire German army (now in excess of half a million men), so clearly the French had to be prepared for a serious military confrontation, not a police action as is sometimes suggested. As it happens, the French general staff was wholly disinclined to act. Apart from the fact that the chief of staff, General Gamelin, had 'no guts' (according to a colleague), the general staff exaggerated the problem by grossly inflating the

Key question
Could Hitler have been stopped in the Rhineland in 1936?

Key date
Hitler moved troops into the Rhineland: 7 March 1936

Key term
Fait accompli
A French phrase meaning a thing already done and not reversible.

German soldiers enter the Rhineland by crossing the bridge at Cologne in March 1936.

estimate of German forces involved in the operation; this was put at the ludicrously high figure of 265,000. To combat this force the army required mobilisation. The French government at that time, which was in any case temporary pending an election in May, could not seriously contemplate war. Moreover, political parties, the press and trade unions all agreed that there should be no war over the Rhineland.

The French government turned to Britain, where the general view was that the Germans were only marching into 'their own backgarden'. Britain acted to restrain the French, who clearly needed little restraining. Was this the last chance to stop Hitler without war? The only option open to France seems to have been to stop Hitler by war, not without war. Whether or not France could have won this war is a moot point. Pope Pius XI thought so, but unfortunately no one listened to him. It is interesting to note that even Churchill was not calling for firm action in March 1936, despite what he said and wrote later. There may well have been an opportunity to topple Hitler at this point, but given the lack of political will on both sides of the English Channel to use force to do so, it remains forever a remote **hypothesis**.

Key term

Hypothesis
A supposition, not necessarily a truth.

A 1936 British cartoon about the Rhineland reoccupation which indicates the German military has torn up the Locarno Pact. The Latin phrase *Pax Germanica*, which means 'German peace', is clearly used ironically: the action is obviously not peaceful at all – it is highly provocative.

Dr Josef Goebbels was Hitler's Minister for Public Enlightenment and Propaganda. Seen here making a speech in 1928.

Key dates

Outbreak of Spanish
Civil War: 18 July 1936

Rome–Berlin Axis:
1 November 1936

Anti-Comintern Pact:
24 November 1936

Key terms

Spanish Civil War
The conflict between
Nationalists and
Republicans fought
in Spain between
1936 and 1939.

Protocols
Draft of terms of
agreement.

Rome–Berlin Axis
A series of
understandings
agreed between
Nazi Germany and
Fascist Italy in 1936.

**Anti-Comintern
Pact**
Originally an
agreement between
Germany and Japan
signed in 1936
which stated both
countries' hostility
to international
communism.

The gamble pays off

The remilitarisation of the Rhineland was a tremendous boost for
Hitler, in terms of both his popularity (he achieved a 99 per cent
approval rating in the 29 March plebiscite) and his self-
confidence. He had acted boldly in the face of foreign office and
army vacillation and had been shown to be right. Goebbels noted:
'The *Führer* beaming. England remains passive. France takes no
action on its own.' Indeed, he had exposed the exclusively
defensive nature of French thinking and this had serious
consequences for France's allies. Belgium immediately renounced
its alliance and in October reverted to neutral status. There was
concern in Eastern Europe too.

But it is really the boost to Hitler's self-belief that was the most
important consequence. He came to believe he had an infallible
political instinct and was destined to carry out his plans. He
increasingly moved from opportunity to intent, that is to say,
instead of reacting to events he now came to mould them, or at
least acted decisively when unexpected opportunities arose.

Hitler and Mussolini

The growing reconciliation between Mussolini and Hitler will be
the subject of the next chapter. Suffice it to say here that in July
Hitler's formal (and insincere) acknowledgement of Austrian
independence and his decision to intervene in the **Spanish Civil
War** on the side of General Franco (as did Mussolini) drew the
dictators together and culminated in October in the signing of a
series of **protocols** that became known as the **Rome–Berlin Axis**,
the first tentative step towards a full military alliance between
Nazi Germany and Fascist Italy. Later, in November, Hitler signed
an agreement with Japan, the **Anti-Comintern Pact**. On the
surface this seemed nothing more than a propaganda ploy, but
the agreement did hold out the prospect of closer co-operation in
the future.

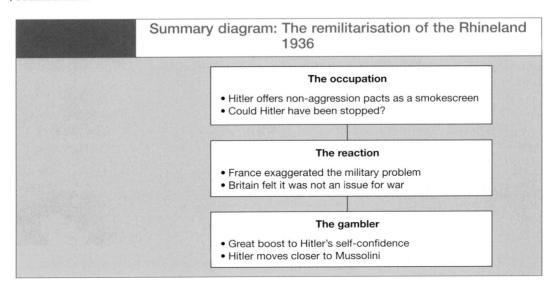

Summary diagram: The remilitarisation of the Rhineland
1936

The occupation
• Hitler offers non-aggression pacts as a smokescreen
• Could Hitler have been stopped?

The reaction
• France exaggerated the military problem
• Britain felt it was not an issue for war

The gambler
• Great boost to Hitler's self-confidence
• Hitler moves closer to Mussolini

5 | The Four-Year Plan

In general, German policy after March 1936 gradually became more strident. Clearly the Abyssinian crisis – which had led to a break between Fascist Italy and the democracies of Britain and France (see page 54) – had improved Germany's diplomatic position, but it was also the case that its military strength was increasing. In August 1936 military service was extended to a period of 2 years and the following month, at the **Nuremberg Rally**, Hitler introduced the Four-Year Plan, which was formally launched under the leadership of Hermann Göring, Hitler's deputy, a month after that.

Schacht and recovery

The revitalisation of the German economy was essential for rapid rearmament, which in turn would enable Hitler to carry out his foreign policy. However, the German economy had still been in serious difficulties in 1933 and rearmament had to be relatively modest in the first 3 years. It seems clear that when he was appointed Chancellor in January 1933, Hitler had no very clear idea about the kind of economic policy he would follow. However, one of his most important early decisions was to appoint Dr Hjalmar Schacht as President of the *Reichsbank*, and later in 1934 as Minister of Finance, to solve the balance of payments problem.

Schacht was, above all, a brilliant financier and he now devoted his considerable talents to the economic consolidation of the Nazi regime and, in particular, to facilitating the start of the rearmament programme. He did this by **deficit financing** and kept it secret by selling so-called 'mefo-bills', which were a type of **government bond**.

During 1934–6 mefo-bills accounted for 50 per cent of arms expenditure (thereafter as the economy recovered, and the need for secrecy decreased, it became possible to finance rearmament from government loans and taxation). However, rapid rearmament was not possible and the little that did occur created a serious balance of payments problem as it sucked in imports of raw materials; at the same time Germany also had to import foodstuffs as its own agriculture only met about 80 per cent of the country's needs, hence the difficult choice between 'guns or butter'.

In a speech in Berlin in January 1936 Goebbels stated: 'We can manage without butter but not, for example, without guns. If we are attacked we can only defend ourselves with guns not with butter.' And later in Hamburg Hermann Göring stated: 'We have no butter … but I ask you – would you rather have butter or guns? … preparedness makes us powerful. Butter merely makes us fat.'

Key question
What can we learn about Hitler's intentions from the Four-Year Plan?

Key date
Four-Year Plan formally launched: 19 October 1936

Key question
How successful had Nazi economic recovery been?

Key terms

Nuremberg Rally
From the late 1920s the Nazi Party held annual political rallies in the city.

Deficit financing
A means of conducting the economy in which government spends more money than it receives as revenue by borrowing in order to stimulate growth.

Government bond
A means of raising money: a certificate issued by a government promising to repay borrowed money at a fixed rate of interest at a specified time.

Dr Hjalmar Schacht (1877–1970) had a remarkable career. He not only was instrumental in placing the Nazi economy on a sound footing, but also had played a key role in the recovery of Weimar after the hyperinflation of 1923, and later, after exoneration at Nuremberg in 1946, was to play an important role in the recovery of West Germany.

Key question
Why was Hitler dissatisfied with the pace of rearmament?

The launch of the Four-Year Plan

By early 1936 the armaments industry was only operating at 70 per cent of capacity because Germany could not afford the raw materials required. Rearmament had not exactly stalled, but it was not on course. And yet by late 1936 the economy had largely recovered. Hitler therefore decided to bring the economy more closely under party control. Some time in August 1936 he composed a memorandum launching the Four-Year Plan – a plan to make Germany ready to wage war. In this document he talked of the forthcoming struggle with Bolshevism and Jewry and the need to develop the economy to be ready to face the danger, in particular the need to develop synthetic raw materials and become self-sufficient. He finished by stating:

> Nearly 4 precious years have gone by. There is no doubt that by now we could have been completely independent of foreign countries in the spheres of fuel supplies, rubber supplies, and partly also iron ore supplies. … There has been enough time in

4 years to find out what we cannot do. Now we have to carry out what we can do.

I thus set the following tasks:

i) The German armed forces must be operational within 4 years.

ii) The German economy must be fit for war within 4 years.

Fourth anniversary

This last point would imply a readiness for war by 1940, but by simply looking at armaments expenditure it is hard to determine exactly what kind of war Hitler had in mind. On 4 September 1936 Hermann Göring, Commander-in-Chief of the *Luftwaffe*, read out Hitler's memorandum to the cabinet stating that he, Göring, would be responsible for executing the plan. The priority the plan had over the economy soon led to a clash with the Minister of Finance, who felt that the pace of rearmament was too quick and the investment in synthetic raw materials uneconomical. In November 1937 Schacht resigned. Most observers felt that he was right, and that by 1939 a serious economic crisis was just around the corner. Such disproportionate expenditure on armaments would lead to a serious imbalance in the economy.

Hermann Göring (1893–1946). A First World War fighter ace, Göring became a Nazi in 1922. He held a number of positions in government and was in charge of the economy after 1936, although he is mainly remembered as the head of the German air force, the *Luftwaffe*. In 1939 he was named as Hitler's successor, but the disappointing performance of the air force in the war led to a fall in his prestige. He was arraigned at the Nuremberg Trials, but cheated the noose by taking poison. In this 1935 photograph he is attending a Nazi mass meeting in the Berlin Sport Palace.

But that crisis was in the future. On 30 January 1937, the fourth anniversary of his accession to power, Hitler addressed the *Reichstag* proclaiming 'the withdrawal of the German signature' from the Versailles Treaty and spoke with pride of his achievements since coming to power. He also stated that 'the time of so-called weekend surprises has been ended' (a reference to the Saturday occupation of the Rhineland), and in truth there were no 'weekend surprises' in 1937. Hitler later referred to 1937 as the 'year of awareness' in the sense of his final recognition that he would have to shelve the idea of a British alliance and strengthen the Italian one.

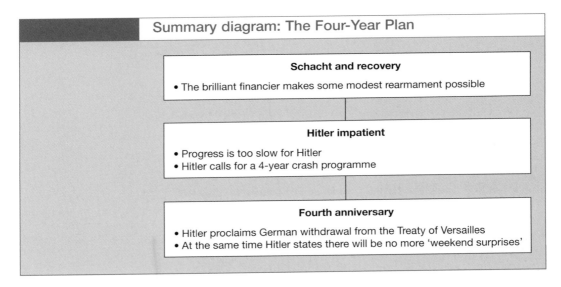

Summary diagram: The Four-Year Plan

Schacht and recovery

• The brilliant financier makes some modest rearmament possible

Hitler impatient

• Progress is too slow for Hitler
• Hitler calls for a 4-year crash programme

Fourth anniversary

• Hitler proclaims German withdrawal from the Treaty of Versailles
• At the same time Hitler states there will be no more 'weekend surprises'

<table>
<tr><td>

Key question

How much of German foreign policy between 1933 and 1937 was continuity and how much of it was of Hitler's own making?

</td></tr>
</table>

6 | Conclusion 1933–6

Continuity?

You now have to make a judgement about Hitler's early foreign policy. You might decide that it did not reveal anything unusual; for instance, it did not reveal his ideological aims. Indeed, you might identify remarkable continuity with the policy of the previous Weimar Republic; after all, armament restrictions had been ignored and reparations effectively ended prior to Hitler's coming to power. Moreover, Nazi policy at this stage reflected the wishes of the armed forces, the foreign ministry and all who wished to reverse Versailles. It was not controversial.

Change?

So, if there was nothing out of the ordinary in Hitler's policy, was his approach in some way different? Here you might be able to identify a change. If we talk about Hitler proceeding with caution in these years, as most historians do, then it should be appreciated that this caution was only relative to what came later. What often characterised Hitler's behaviour was considerable boldness and an ability to take opportunities that others might not have dared to take. This has been described as the gambler's instinct, but might more reasonably be explained by reference to Hitler's self-belief, his strength of will, his unshakeable certainty that the future would bring the fulfilment of his own world philosophy. He was clearly a man with aims who was not prepared just to react to events, as the democracies seem to have done.

In a very short space of time he had left the Disarmament Conference and the League of Nations, broken off relations with the Soviets, encouraged the Austrian Nazis (although not in the assassination of Dollfuss), accelerated the pace of rearmament, denounced the Versailles Treaty's armament limitations, reintroduced conscription and reoccupied the Rhineland. Not exactly the moves of a moderate.

Skill or luck?

If Hitler had shown great boldness, he had also shown great skill and had enjoyed not a little luck. After all, the success he enjoyed when he left the League and Conference (blaming the French) was, to some extent, lost when the Austrian Chancellor was assassinated, albeit on local initiative and not on orders from Berlin. However, the initiative was restored quite by coincidence, by the Saar plebiscite. The area was Catholic and industrial and therefore not a haven of traditional Nazi support, and the vote was free. Therefore the overwhelming pro-German result was a much needed boost for Hitler's prestige at home and abroad.

Hitler was also clever in his use of propaganda, especially when he reintroduced conscription in 1935. In this matter he was able to cite British and French rearmament plans as the main reason. In 1936 he remilitarised the Rhineland at a time when the democracies were preoccupied with the Abyssinian crisis. He seems to have been able to take a bold move and get away with it. All this led to a feeling of popular exhilaration in Germany and fed his growing self-confidence.

Amoral?

Of course you might identify another advantage that Hitler had, and that was his **amoral** position. He was prepared to say or do anything to get his own way. Hitler always tried to defuse potentially dangerous situations by saying all the things that peaceful people wanted to hear. He always coupled a bold move with some offer of peace. In addition, he made the Non-Aggression Pact with Poland against the advice of his foreign office because it meant nothing to him, and he offered a naval agreement to Britain just at the right moment, despite the opposition of the navy, because the quotas also meant nothing to him. He also guaranteed Austrian independence; again because it was what Mussolini wanted to hear.

Hitler seemed to be a good judge of his opponents, realising that they would leap at bilateral agreements even though **concert diplomacy** was their aim. Of course, many politicians are prepared to bend or at least be 'economical' with the truth, but what set Hitler apart was his almost complete disregard for the truth.

Amoral
Having no moral principles at all.

Concert diplomacy
A process or method whereby general agreement of all the major powers is reached.

Key terms

Stepping stones to glory. David Low implies in this cartoon published in the London *Evening Standard* in 1936 that Hitler is taking advantage of the weak governments of the West in order to get his own way.

The point is that for Hitler treaties were simply a means to an end, to be signed and then discarded as circumstances dictated. Hitler was able to adopt this approach because he did have ends: concrete goals, as we have indicated in the early part of this chapter. And so you might conclude that although Hitler's ideology was not revealed in his early foreign policy, it was nevertheless its driving force. That is to say, policy was driven by Hitler's messianic self-belief that **providence** (his term) had placed him on this Earth to destroy Versailles, unite all Germans and create a Greater German Empire in the East, and this could only be achieved by war. But we must not make out that Hitler was cleverer than he really was; he was in fact operating in a most favourable international climate.

The context

- As we have indicated, throughout the interwar period France was growing weaker, both politically and economically, and relied on Britain to maintain the *status quo*.
- Britain, like France, was pacific, but prepared to make some modifications to the Versailles Treaty. Britain was also not in a strong position as it had too many commitments and too few resources and was, in any case, largely preoccupied with imperial responsibilities.
- At the same time, Stalin's main concern was to avoid war at all costs: the Soviet Union had just embarked on a series of 5-year plans to modernise the economy and catch up with the other powers.

Key question
To what extent was Hitler operating in favourable circumstances?

Key terms

Providence
The protective care of God or nature.

Status quo
The existing state of affairs.

- Italy enjoyed a diplomatic position of some importance that far exceeded its actual power. This was mainly due to the blusterings of *Il Duce*, Mussolini. However, Italy too was a revisionist, expansionist power and Mussolini was eager to build up the Italian Empire, in the **Balkans** and particularly in Africa.
- Japan had already shown with its invasion of Manchuria in 1931 (see page 18) that the League of Nations could be ignored and Britain was particularly worried about Japanese expansionism …
- … as indeed was the USA. However, the world's most powerful nation was concerned not to be drawn into an active foreign policy at this time.

Balkans
The countries that occupy the peninsula in south-eastern Europe bound by the Adriatic and Ionian Seas in the west, by the Aegean in the east, and the Mediterranean in the south, i.e. Greece, Albania, Yugoslavia, Bulgaria, Romania and Turkey.

Key term

The omens for Hitler were therefore good. Britain was pacific and amenable, France weak, Russia preoccupied, Italy dissatisfied and the USA in virtual isolation. Moreover within Germany Hitler had considerable support. As has been stated, although Hitler's approach to foreign policy was very much of his own making, clearly the army and industrialists were very much in favour of rearmament, the foreign ministry wished for the overthrow of the Versailles Treaty and the mass of German people longed for the restoration of German prestige. There was, therefore, a considerable identity of interest that gave Hitler the green light to deal with the unfinished business of the First World War. Given Hitler's personality, this domestic climate and his ideological aims, the pressure for continued initiatives, for greater successes, could only gather momentum.

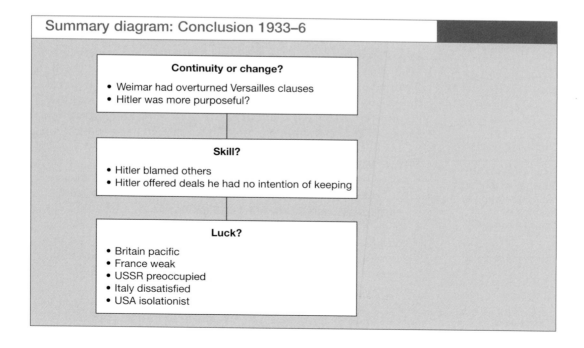

Summary diagram: Conclusion 1933–6

Continuity or change?
- Weimar had overturned Versailles clauses
- Hitler was more purposeful?

Skill?
- Hitler blamed others
- Hitler offered deals he had no intention of keeping

Luck?
- Britain pacific
- France weak
- USSR preoccupied
- Italy dissatisfied
- USA isolationist

Study Guide: Advanced-level Questions
In the style of Edexcel
In the paper you are given an hour to write a single essay for which 60 marks are awarded. There will be a choice of two questions. Here are three relevant to the chapter you have just read.

(a) 'By 1937 Hitler could rightly claim he had successfully challenged the most damaging restrictions placed on Germany by the Treaty of Versailles.' How far do you agree with this judgement?

Source: Edexcel, June 2003

(b) 'It was the boldness displayed by Hitler in the years 1933–6 that explains his success in challenging the Versailles Settlement.' How far do you agree with this judgement?

Source: Edexcel, January 2004

(c) 'Favourable circumstances, rather than diplomatic skill, explain why Germany enjoyed such success in foreign policy in the years 1933–6.' How far do you agree with this judgement?

Source: Edexcel, January 2002

Exam tips

The cross-references are intended to take you straight to the material that will help you to answer the questions.

You should use your introduction to an essay to address the question, define its terms where necessary and in effect answer it by explaining your view. The rest of the essay should then be used to justify the position you have taken at the beginning by developing the argument with relevant factual support. Remember that the greatest enemy of the effective essay is irrelevance: hence you should be addressing the question at all times, as often as not in an explicit sense, though not in a mechanical fashion. By the time you reach your conclusion you should have the marks in the bag.

(a) This is not an easy question.

- First of all you must be familiar with the terms of the Treaty of Versailles (page 10).
- Secondly, you have to decide which terms were the most damaging. For instance, if you decide that reparations and the creation of the Polish corridor were the most damaging then Hitler had not been successful: reparations had ceased prior to his coming to power (page 19) and he had done nothing about Poland. On the other hand, if you consider the armament limitations and the demilitarisation of the Rhineland as most damaging, then clearly Hitler had been successful (see pages 31, 32 and 36).
- Obviously you will need to pick your way between the two positions here and reach a balanced evaluation that will enable you to determine 'how far' you agree with the judgement.

(b) This question requires you to:

- identify Hitler's success in challenging the Versailles settlement (pages 31, 32 and 36)
- identify Hitler's 'boldness' in accounting for that success (pages 39 and 44)
- identify other factors: opponents' weaknesses, a favourable diplomatic environment, etc. (pages 45 and 46)
- weigh all of them up to reach a reasoned judgement.

(c) Similarly, with question **(c)**, you need to:

- identify Hitler's foreign policy successes (this is broader than just the Versailles Treaty)
- evaluate the favourable circumstances
- evaluate Hitler's skill
- weigh up the two given factors
- consider other factors
- reach a reasoned judgement.

3

The Diplomatic Revolution: Hitler and Mussolini 1933–9

POINTS TO CONSIDER
This chapter will take you through the remarkable transformation in relations between Hitler and Mussolini, from a frosty start to a full-blown military alliance. How did this come about? The key areas examined are:

- Hitler and Mussolini: a frosty start
- The invasion of Abyssinia 1935
- From Axis to alliance 1936–9
- Conclusion 1933–9

Key dates

1933	October 14	Hitler left the League of Nations
1934	June 14–15	Hitler visited Mussolini
	July 25	Chancellor Dollfuss of Austria assassinated
	December 5–6	Wal-Wal incident
	December 30	Mussolini issued orders for the conquest of Abyssinia
1935	January 7	'Rome Accords' signed between France and Italy
	October 3	Italy invaded Abyssinia
	December 8	Hoare–Laval Plan
1936	March 7	Hitler remilitarised the Rhineland
	May 5	Addis Ababa fell
	July 18	Outbreak of Spanish Civil War
	November 1	Rome–Berlin Axis announced
1937	September	Mussolini visited Hitler
	November 6	Italy joined the Anti-Comintern Pact
	December 11	Italy left the League
1938	March 12	Hitler moved into Austria
	September 29	Munich Conference
1939	March 14–15	Hitler marched into Prague
	March 28	Spanish Civil War ended
	April 7	Italy seized Albania
	May 22	Pact of Steel signed
	August 23	Nazi–Soviet Pact
	September 1	Germany invaded Poland
	September 3	Britain and France declared war on Germany
1940	June 10	Mussolini declared war on Britain and France

1 | Hitler and Mussolini: A Frosty Start

What enabled Hitler to pursue his aims with greater confidence and flexibility was the diplomatic revolution that occurred in the mid-1930s. The main cause of this change was the Italian dictator, Benito Mussolini, whose actions over Abyssinia (now called Ethiopia) led to a split with the democracies and reconciliation with Germany. To begin with, however, relations between **Fascist** Italy and **Nazi** Germany were not good, despite the obvious ideological affinity.

It should be remembered that when Hitler took office in January 1933, Mussolini had already been in power for over a decade and was a leader of some standing. Indeed Hitler had a genuine admiration for *Il Duce* and on his first day in office sent him a message expressing his 'strong admiration and homage' for him, and pointing out that he would never have succeeded without Mussolini's example. Mussolini did not reciprocate. Indeed he seems to have held Hitler in low regard, disliked his fanaticism and often referred to him as '*quel pazzo*' ('that madman').

Mussolini felt that Hitler's anti-Semitism was positively medieval and disliked the way the Nazis had copied his movement. Moreover, he was furious when Hitler walked out of both the disarmament talks and the League of Nations (see page 28). He well knew that Germany's leader, an Austrian by birth, had designs on Austria, Italy's vulnerable neighbour. So, in March 1934 by the 'Rome Protocols' Mussolini emphasised Italian support for both Austria and Hungary; however, he could not generate any British or French support for this policy and became pessimistic about it. Accordingly, in June he finally agreed to a meeting with Hitler which took place near Venice. Although these matters have been referred to in the previous chapter, they are worth reiterating in this context.

The Austrian crisis

Hitler's meeting with Mussolini did not go well, and the following month when Austrian Nazis murdered the Austrian Chancellor, Dollfuss – when Dollfuss's wife was actually staying with the Mussolini family – relations hit rock bottom. Mussolini took the matter personally and rushed four **divisions** to the **Brenner Pass** to assist the new Austrian government in the event of a Nazi coup. Hitler, who probably knew nothing of the planned assassination, backed down from any attempt to take advantage of the situation. From this point on he became a legitimate figure of abuse in Italy, often depicted as a clown. Mussolini, on the other hand, emerged from the crisis with his prestige enhanced. He had saved Austria, stood up to Hitler, and thereby earned the admiration of both Britain and France. He now hoped to get some form of tangible reward from the democracies, and in January 1935 the French signed a firm agreement – the 'Rome Accords' – and handed over some territory in Africa adjacent to both Libya and Eritrea.

Key question
Why did Italo-German relations get off to such a bad start?

Key dates

Hitler left the League of Nations:
14 October 1933

Hitler visited Mussolini:
14–15 June 1934

Chancellor Dollfuss of Austria assassinated:
25 July 1934

'Rome Accords' signed between France and Italy:
7 January 1935

Key terms

Fascist
'Fascism' derives from the Latin *fasces*, which were a bundle of rods carried as a symbol of power in ancient Rome; accordingly, the Fascist Party, which Mussolini founded in 1919, was authoritarian, nationalist and right-wing.

Nazi
Nazi is simply an abbreviation of the German for 'National Socialist German Workers' Party'.

Divisions
Groups of army brigades, each numbering about 10,000–15,000 men.

Brenner Pass
An Alpine pass on the Austro-Italian border.

Profile: Benito Mussolini 1883–1945

1883	–	Born in Predappio in the Romagna
1907	–	Qualified as a teacher
1912	–	Editor of the Socialist Party newspaper *Avanti!*
1914	–	Supported the war. Expelled from the Socialist Party. Founded his own newspaper *Il Popolo d'Italia*
1915–17	–	Served in the war and was wounded
1919	–	Founded the Fascist movement
1922	–	Became Prime Minister
1929	–	Signed **Lateran Accords** with Papacy
1935	–	Invaded Abyssinia
1936	–	Intervened in the Spanish Civil War. Rome–Berlin Axis (see page 59)
1939	–	Invaded Albania. Pact of Steel (see page 64)
1940	–	Declared war on Britain and France
1943	–	Dismissed by the king, but was installed as leader of the Italian Social Republic by the Germans
1945	–	Shot by partisans

Key term

Lateran Accords
A treaty signed in 1929 between Mussolini and Pope Pius XI recognising the Vatican as a sovereign state.

Mussolini started out as a socialist and was a successful journalist; however, he served in the war and split with the socialists over this issue as they were opposed to any participation in the conflict. After the war in 1919 he founded the Fascist movement and became violently anti-socialist. He came to power in 1922 and gradually established himself as the dictator of a one-party state.

Mussolini's aim was to make Italy 'great, respected and feared' as he put it, and every Italian was to become a good Fascist. His theme of a link with the ancient Roman Empire was made manifest in his expansionist foreign policy, with the occupation of Abyssinia (1935) and Albania (1939). He formed the Axis with Germany (1936) and aided Franco's Spain. At what he deemed to be the most favourable moment with France and Britain seemingly beaten (1940) he entered the Second World War, but met with disaster everywhere; he was no Caesar and his soldiers were not heirs to the Roman legionaries. Although he had been popular at the time of the Lateran Accords with the Pope (1929), and at the time of the invasion of Abyssinia (1935) and the peacemaking in Munich (1938), he was discarded by the Italian people in 1943. He was rescued by the Germans and ruled a puppet republic in the north of Italy, but as the Allies closed in he was shot by Italian partisans on 28 April 1945 when trying to flee.

However, what Mussolini really wanted was a free hand in Abyssinia and a firm alliance in Europe. Pierre Laval, the new French Foreign Minister, did give an ambiguous verbal assurance that the French government would turn a blind eye to Italian activities in Abyssinia, but this did not amount to an endorsement for invasion. And yet by this time Mussolini was already committed to a war of conquest.

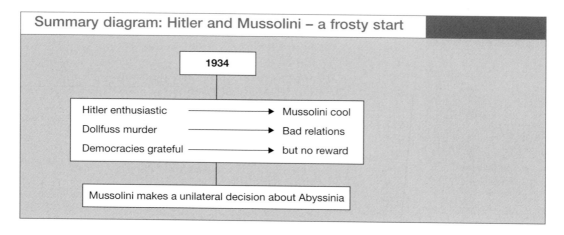

Summary diagram: Hitler and Mussolini – a frosty start

1934

Hitler enthusiastic	→	Mussolini cool
Dollfuss murder	→	Bad relations
Democracies grateful	→	but no reward

Mussolini makes a unilateral decision about Abyssinia

2 | The Invasion of Abyssinia 1935

Background

The Italian state had long wished to possess Abyssinia, but had been humiliated by defeat by the native tribesmen at Adowa in 1896. Nevertheless, in 1906 Britain and France had recognised the area as an Italian **sphere of influence**. However, Italy gained little in the **'mutilated' peace of 1919** and its frustrated colonial ambitions soured relations with the democracies in the post-war period. Italy tried to win over Abyssinia by friendship in the 1920s, sponsoring its membership of the League of Nations in 1924 against British and French objections, and signing a treaty of friendship in 1928. However, this policy was unsuccessful and by the 1930s Mussolini was getting impatient. The possibility of an invasion had been discussed as early as 1925, but actual plans were not drawn up until 1932.

Mussolini wished to conquer Abyssinia for a variety of reasons:

- to avenge the defeat of 1896
- for prestige
- as an outlet for Italian colonists
- as a source of recruits for the army
- for its economic value
- imperial aggrandisement.

The last point was probably the fundamental motive. Mussolini was obsessed with the idea of reconstituting the Roman Empire, albeit in a place where the Caesars had never been. And the timing had a lot to do with Hitler's coming to power. A powerful Germany was seen as a threat initially, and Mussolini felt he had to move before Hitler tried for Austria again.

Position of Britain and France

Italy was not a strong power: it lacked basic industrial raw materials such as coal and iron. That Italy enjoyed a position of some diplomatic stature was largely due to the efforts of Mussolini, who exaggerated Italy's capabilities at every opportunity, and Hitler's coming to power, which unnerved the democracies.

Key question
Why did Mussolini invade Abyssinia?

Sphere of influence
The claimed or recognised area of a state's interests.

'Mutilated' peace of 1919
Although allied to Austria and Germany in the First World War, Italy had joined in on the side of Britain and France by the Treaty of London in 1915. In this treaty Italy was made a number of promises that it would gain territory in the Balkans and colonies. However, Italy received very little in 1919.

Key terms

Key question
What was the British and French attitude to Italian ambitions in Abyssinia?

Accordingly, as we have already seen, by the 1930s France was contemplating giving Italy a free hand in Abyssinia. However, although it had been perfectly acceptable to carve Africa up prior to 1914, in the post-war world new rules applied. Some might say that this was because Britain and France had already acquired what they wanted and were therefore prepared to pay lip-service to the USA's anti-colonial stance. Colonial conquest had therefore simply become unfashionable, unacceptable to many and even immoral to some. Moreover, Italy had mistakenly made Abyssinia a member of the League of Nations, with all the rights that go with membership.

The 'Stresa Front' of April 1935 (see page 34) boosted *Il Duce*'s confidence, and in June France and Italy signed a secret treaty to guarantee Austrian independence. Britain, on the other hand, was categorically not prepared to offer Mussolini a free hand in Abyssinia – the League of Nations and the concept of **collective security** were very popular with the British electorate – but the government did want to remain on good terms with the Italian dictator and said nothing about the matter at Stresa. Mussolini himself intercepted an internal Foreign Office assessment that stated that Britain had no vital interests in Abyssinia. This, however, was not the same as sanctioning an invasion.

Invasion

In any event, Mussolini decided to invade. Already in December 1934 an incident at **Wal-Wal** in which a number of Italian soldiers were killed had been used to justify retaliation and throughout 1935 military preparations went ahead. Then on 2 October 1935 Mussolini gave a speech in which he stated:

> When in 1915 Italy exposed itself to the risks of war and joined its destiny with that of the Allies, how much praise there was for our courage and how many promises were made! But after the common victory to which Italy had made the supreme contribution of 670,000 dead, 400,000 mutilated, and a million wounded, around the hateful peace table Italy received but a few crumbs from the rich colonial booty gathered by others.
>
> We have been patient for 13 years, during which the circle of selfishness that strangles our vitality has become even tighter. With Abyssinia we have been patient for 40 years! It is time to say enough!

The next day Italy invaded Abyssinia. The actual campaign does not concern us here, but suffice it to say that the use of aircraft and poisoned gas on poorly armed tribesmen, together with nearly half a million soldiers eventually enabled Italy to prevail. Even so, the capital, Addis Ababa, was not taken until May 1936 and it took a further 3 years of considerable brutality to subdue the entire population. The cost of the campaign was enormous. Abyssinia proved to be an economic millstone and Italy was thereby seriously weakened thereafter. The most significant consequences, however, were the diplomatic ones.

Key terms

Collective security
The idea that all the powers would band together against an aggressor.

Wal-Wal
A skirmish at an oasis 80 km inside Abyssinia where the Italians had set up a garrison, claiming the area to be Italian territory.

Key question
Why did Mussolini feel justified in taking this action?

Key dates

Wal-Wal incident: 5–6 December 1934

Mussolini issued orders for the conquest of Abyssinia: 30 December 1934

Italy invaded Abyssinia: 3 October 1935

Addis Ababa fell: 5 May 1936

Consequences

It was an election year in Britain and, therefore, the government was quick to take the initiative in imposing League **sanctions** on Italy; France reluctantly followed. The sanctions were half-hearted – oil was excluded and the Suez Canal remained open (either one could have crippled the campaign) – but sufficient to cause some difficulty to the Italian economy and considerable irritation to Mussolini. This was the public policy; in private a negotiated settlement was attempted. Britain wanted a League policy to please the electorate, but also wanted to avoid a breach with Italy. The result was disastrous as neither policy was pursued to a successful conclusion, as *Punch* magazine sarcastically pointed out.

In private Britain and France attempted a compromise scheme: the **Hoare–Laval Plan** of December 1935. However, the plan was leaked to the French press and the resulting furore caused it to be

Key question
Why was Anglo-French policy so indecisive?

Sanctions
Military or economic penalties imposed to coerce a state to conform to international agreement.

Hoare–Laval Plan
Sir Samuel Hoare, British Foreign Secretary, and Pierre Laval, French Foreign Secretary, drew up a secret deal whereby Italy would be given about two-thirds of Abyssinia.

THE AWFUL WARNING.

FRANCE AND ENGLAND
(*together ?*).

"WE DON'T WANT YOU TO FIGHT,
BUT, BY JINGO, IF YOU DO,
WE SHALL PROBABLY ISSUE A JOINT MEMORANDUM
SUGGESTING A MILD DISAPPROVAL OF YOU."

The *Punch* cartoon of 1935 contains a variation on the original 'jingo' music-hall song first sung in 1878, when Britain confronted Russia over the creation of a large slav state in the Balkans and forced her to back down:

We don't want to fight;
But, by jingo, if we do,
We've got the men,
We've got the ships,
We've got the money too.

Clearly the parody in *Punch* was meant to highlight the contrast with the original, somewhat more aggressive lyrics.

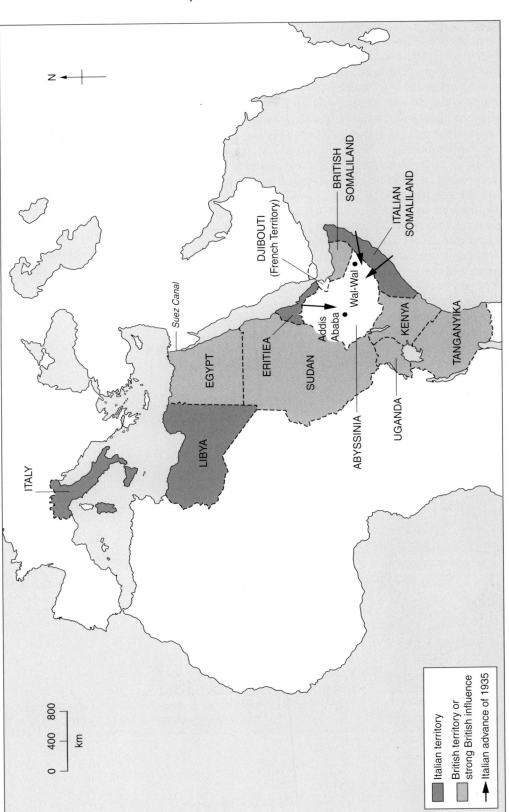

British, French and Italian possessions in eastern Africa.

scrapped. In any event Mussolini would have settled for nothing less than the whole of Abyssinia. His success in this matter – in conquering the African colony, in defying the League and in effect outmanoeuvring Britain – made him enormously popular at home. This proved to be the peak of his success. He now came to despise the democracies for what he felt was their betrayal; he could not understand why Italy had been singled out for sanctions when neither Japan nor Germany had been – and both had defied the League.

Already in 1935 Mussolini had contemplated closer relations with Germany; in 1936 he realised 'only a **revanchist** Germany would back the Italian challenge to Anglo-French **hegemony** in the Mediterranean and help Italy become a Great Power'. Italo-German relations now underwent a rapid improvement, to such an extent that Hitler was able to use the Abyssinian crisis as a cover to carry out the remilitarisation of the Rhineland a year in advance of his intentions (see page 36).

Thus, Abyssinia proved to be a significant turning point in European affairs. If Manchuria (see page 18) had begun the decline of the League, Abyssinia brought about its eclipse (all subsequent crises were handled outside the League structure); Germany had at last come out of isolation; and the democracies were in disarray. All this worked in Hitler's favour; he was the real beneficiary of the Abyssinian war.

Key date

Hitler remilitarised the Rhineland: 7 March 1936

Key terms

Revanchist
Revengeful.

Hegemony
Leadership especially by one country.

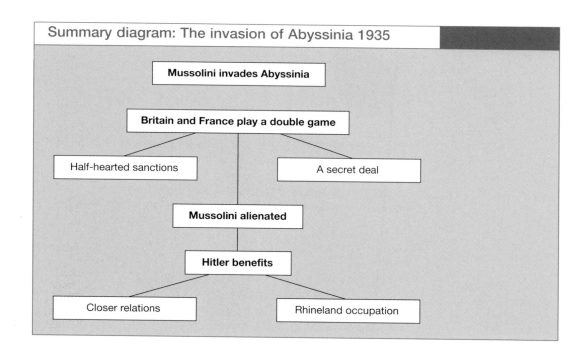

Summary diagram: The invasion of Abyssinia 1935

- Mussolini invades Abyssinia
- Britain and France play a double game
  - Half-hearted sanctions
  - A secret deal
- Mussolini alienated
- Hitler benefits
  - Closer relations
  - Rhineland occupation

3 | From Axis to Alliance 1936–9

Key question
What brought the Italian and German dictators closer together?

Mussolini was alarmed and surprised at Hitler's move into the Rhineland, but it reinforced his interest in a German alliance. Although he had come to see that Fascist ideology was creating a common link between the two countries, he was more impressed by German power and wanted to be on the winning side in any forthcoming conflict. On 1 April 1936, he ordered the Italian press to become pro-German and in June he appointed the pro-German Galeazzo Ciano (his son-in-law) as foreign minister. Mussolini took comfort from the agreement between Germany and Austria on 11 July, by which Germany acknowledged Austrian independence and in return Austria agreed to pursue a foreign policy in line with German interests, a scheme which *Il Duce* had proposed in January.

Key date

Outbreak of the Spanish Civil War: 18 July 1936

So, just 2 years after his firm pro-Austrian stand, Mussolini had in effect abandoned it.

Hitler was cautious; he still favoured a British alliance and knew that Mussolini, who was keeping his options open, was to some extent playing a double game. However, conversations with London were discouraging (Britain wanted a European rather than a bilateral agreement) and Germany made a point of supplying Italy during the Abyssinian crisis despite the League ban (though Hitler's main concern was to keep the war in Africa going rather than bring it to a swift conclusion). The event which further accelerated the Italo-German **rapprochement** was the outbreak of the Spanish Civil War in July 1936. The nationalist leader, General Franco, appealed to both dictators; and both dictators decided to assist.

Key term

Rapprochement
Resumption of harmonious relations.

Spanish Civil War 1936–9

Key question
What role did this war play in cementing the Rome–Berlin Axis?

Hitler had a number of reasons for intervening in the Spanish Civil War:

- he had an eye on Spain's valuable raw materials
- he wished to test out his air force
- he wanted a pro-German government
- he saw an opportunity to get closer to Italy, and
- he could portray intervention as an anti-Communist crusade.

Ultimately Hitler committed about 600 aircraft to the conflict; Mussolini, on the other hand, sent in a total of 73,000 troops, at great expense. He had been reluctant at first to get involved, but eventually saw involvement as a matter of prestige. A Fascist government in Madrid, he hoped, would be an Italian puppet. Intervention was rationalised as a move against France, as strengthening Italy's strategic position in the Mediterranean, and as an anti-Communist crusade; but in truth Italy got very little in return.

Still, the Spanish Civil War polarised opinion in Europe, confirmed the democracies' weakness in the eyes of those who believed this to be the case (Britain and France adopted a policy of non-intervention), and brought Germany and Italy closer.

Count Galeazzo Ciano (1903–44), seen here at work in 1937, owed his position as foreign minister (1936–43) to the fact that he was Mussolini's son-in-law. At first pro-Nazi then anti-Nazi, later pro-war then anti-war, he played a leading role in Mussolini's dismissal in 1943, but was later executed for this betrayal.

Together the Abyssinian affair and the Spanish Civil War injected a strong note of ideology into international relations, seeming to herald a conflict between Fascism and democracy.

The war begins

The Spanish Civil War began when a group of military conspirators rose against the left-wing government in Spain. The coup was not an immediate success, as some of the army and much of the navy remained loyal to the Republican regime. General Franco, for the Nationalists, needed help to transport 50,000 troops from Morocco. As was mentioned earlier, Mussolini was initially reluctant to help, but Foreign Secretary Ciano, wished to do so, and it was reported that the Germans were sending planes; so he changed his mind.

Mussolini's motives were political rather than military; anti-communism came to be paramount as he saw the Republicans as Communist, and communism as the ideological opposite of Fascism. Italy made no claims on Spanish territory, although Mussolini did express an interest in naval bases in the **Balearics** as these would challenge British and French dominance in the Mediterranean.

Balearics
Collective noun for the islands of Majorca, Minorca and Ibiza.

Key term

Franco meets Mussolini in 1941. From left to right: Suner (Spain's Foreign Minister), Franco and Mussolini. Despite the aid he received from the Axis powers, Franco did not join them in the Second World War. He ruled Spain until his death in 1975.

Intervention was thought to be a short-term commitment and at the beginning there was no thought of a joint Fascist alliance, and yet that is what unexpectedly emerged over the next few weeks. It did not make sense for Germany and Italy to send arms independently without consulting each other, so in August the Germans took the initiative to suggest closer military co-operation. Thus the Rome–Berlin Axis was born in Spain.

Rome–Berlin Axis 1936

In September 1936 Mussolini was invited to Germany. He accepted, but sent Ciano in October to prepare the way. Hitler went out of his way to welcome Ciano and the two men signed a series of secret protocols which outlined their mutual interests: it was agreed that the Mediterranean was an 'Italian lake' and that Germany should have a free hand in Central and Eastern Europe. On 1 November Mussolini made a speech in Milan coining the phrase 'Rome–Berlin Axis':

> One great country has recently gathered a vast amount of sympathy among the Italian people; I speak of Germany. The meeting at Berlin resulted in an agreement between the two countries on certain questions. … But these agreements which have been included in special statements and signed – this vertical line between Rome and Berlin is not a partition, but rather an axis

Key question
What sort of agreement was the Rome–Berlin Axis?

Key date
Rome–Berlin Axis announced:
1 November 1936

around which all the European states animated by the will to
collaboration and peace can also collaborate. Germany, although
surrounded and solicited, did not adhere to sanctions. With the
agreement of 11 July there disappeared any element of dissension
between Berlin and Rome, and I may remind you that even before
the Berlin meeting Germany had practically recognised the Empire
of Rome.

An Italian invention?

The Axis was almost entirely an Italian invention. Naturally Hitler
was delighted, but he had done little to bring it about. However,
the Axis was not yet anything formal, merely a 'special
relationship', and the Germans were still not convinced by Ciano's
assurance that Italy was no longer 'the whore of the democracies'.
Indeed in Mussolini's eyes, it was vague enough to be jettisoned if
need be. But within 18 months, the Axis became for Fascist Italy
an obligation dictated by harsh necessity, from which there was
no exit.

In the meantime Hitler turned his attentions elsewhere. He still
courted Britain, but by sending Joachim von Ribbentrop as
ambassador to London he made a grave mistake (Ribbentrop was
considered a bit of a buffoon), although a bilateral agreement was
never on the cards. Hitler came to see that he was better off with
a newly won-over Italy. And Italian ambitions conveniently
troubled the French.

Franco's slow progress

Italy and Germany had expected that Franco would win a quick
victory, but they were dismayed by his slow progress; accordingly
they stepped up their aid. In practice, Italy became more
involved than Germany, sending troops and ships. Of the
German leaders only Göring, head of the *Luftwaffe*, was keen on
helping Franco, which is why most German support was in the
form of aircraft. Moreover, as time passed, the Axis powers' aims
diverged; whereas Mussolini wanted the war over quickly, Hitler
came to see that the war both distracted world attention from his
designs and kept Mussolini on side; accordingly he was happy to
let Franco take his time.

A disaster for Italy

Throughout 1937 the Spanish conflict dominated European
politics, but in 1938 international interest subsided. Both Britain
and the Soviet Union came to realise that Franco would not join
the Axis, and in any event, the focus of European tension moved
to Central Europe. For Mussolini the war was a disaster: there was
no control (Franco was nobody's poodle) and no glory, just
enormous expense. The war dragged on until Franco was finally
victorious in the spring of 1939.

The Italian Volunteer Corps returned in 'triumph', but the war
had resulted in thousands of dead and wounded soldiers, and at a
cost of 8.5 billion lira. However, what was significant was that the
war had firmly tied Mussolini to the Axis and had constantly kept

Spanish Civil War
ended: 28 March
1939

Key date

him at loggerheads with Britain and France. For his part, Mussolini felt the war confirmed that the democracies were weak, whereas the Germans and Italians were made of sterner stuff: they were willing to fight. But if Spain kept the Axis together, so too did Mussolini's dream of a Mediterranean empire and Hitler's ambitions in Austria.

Anschluss

Mussolini's visit

In September 1937, Mussolini finally came to Germany. To honour his guest, Hitler pulled out all the stops and put on a display of considerable spectacle. Mussolini was suitably impressed. Indeed he was flattered by everyone he met: this was the real recognition that he craved. Putting their first unfortunate meeting at Venice behind them, the two men developed a relationship that endured, although on this occasion they did not spend much time together.

As time wore on, Mussolini fell into the role of the subordinate partner and came more and more under Hitler's spell. He returned to Italy convinced that the future lay with Germany. A few weeks later Italy signed up to the Anti-Comintern Pact and

Key question
Why did Mussolini allow Hitler to annex Austria?

Key dates

Mussolini visited Hitler: September 1937

Italy joined the Anti-Comintern Pact: 6 November 1937

Hitler (left) and Mussolini (right) meeting in Munich in 1937.

At the top, this Soviet cartoon of 1938 gives the message from Moscow that Hitler has already 'caught' Italy, the boot-shaped fish; and now that he is catching Austria, he can dispense with Mussolini. Unlike the Soviet cartoon, the British one from *Punch* below (also 1938) – perhaps unrealistically – sees Mussolini's acquiescence as more significant than Hitler's exploitation of him.

GOOD HUNTING

Mussolini. " All right, Adolf—I never heard a shot "

in December left the League of Nations, to show solidarity with Germany. However, the German alliance came at a price, and that price was Austria.

When Hitler did move in to Austria in March 1938, it was not at a time of his own choosing and Mussolini was not informed in advance (see page 74). However, the latter had little choice but to accept what had happened with as much good grace as he could muster. Hitler was effusively grateful for *Il Duce*'s acquiescence, as this exchange with Prince Philip of Hesse, his emissary in Rome, indicates:

> *Hesse*: I have just come back from the Palazzo Venezia. The *Duce* accepted the whole thing in a very friendly manner. He sends you his regards.
> *Hitler*: Then please tell Mussolini I will never forget him for this.
> *Hesse*: Yes.
> *Hitler*: Never, never, never, whatever happens. As soon as the Austrian affair is settled, I shall be ready to go with him, through thick and thin, no matter what happens.
> *Hesse*: Yes, my *Führer*.

Key dates

Italy left the League: 11 December 1937

Hitler moved into Austria: 12 March 1938

Key terms

Anti-Semitic laws
A series of laws were passed in Italy discriminating against the Jews in the years 1938–9.

Revisionist demands
This refers to Germany's wish to revise the Paris Peace Settlement.

Irredentist
Literally, unredeemed, used in reference to the return of territory lost to France.

However, the *Anschluss* was undoubtedly a prelude to further German moves and no longer could Mussolini or anyone else believe that he was the senior partner in the Axis, or that he could control Hitler. Still, it became an aim of the new British Prime Minister (from mid-1937), Neville Chamberlain, to try to detach Mussolini from Hitler, and with the resignation of the Foreign Secretary, Anthony Eden – hitherto an obstacle – in 1938, the way was open for improved relations. Accordingly, on 16 April 1938 the British finally recognised Italy's conquest of Abyssinia, but that was not enough for the Italian leader. His strategy had been to use the German alliance to threaten Britain and France and so make gains in the Mediterranean, the Middle East and Africa, but this strategy did not really work. Indeed Britain and France remained obstacles to his ambitions in these areas. So, it seemed to him that he had little choice but to remain within the German alliance.

In May 1938 Hitler made a return visit to Rome and although Hitler flattered and admired Mussolini, the two men were not really on the same wavelength; Mussolini was alternately bored, impressed and beaten down by Hitler, and usually ended up agreeing in order to end the meeting. Mussolini turned down a military alliance at this stage, yet went on to imitate aspects of Nazi policy introducing **anti-Semitic laws** and getting the army to adopt a new way of marching, the *passo Romano*, which turned out to be the German goose step. On the international stage, he also parodied the German dictator's **revisionist demands** in Eastern Europe by raising the **irredentist** cry for the French territory of Nice, Corsica and Tunisia.

Munich Conference

By the summer of 1938 the 'Czech problem' came to dominate European diplomacy (see page 76). Mussolini's role in this crisis was minimal until 28 September when he suddenly became a somewhat improbable peacemaker. Chamberlain asked him to persuade Hitler to a conference in Munich. Hitler agreed as the meeting was to give him what he wanted: the Sudetenland. Accordingly, the Germans drew up a list of requirements for the conference which Mussolini presented as his own. On his return to Italy he was met by cheering crowds wherever he went, but his people's overt expression of pacifism disappointed him. In truth, Mussolini's role had been largely artificial: the conference had been Chamberlain's initiative and it was the Germans who formulated the agreement.

In January 1939 Chamberlain visited Mussolini and although the visit was amicable little was achieved. Mussolini's Mediterranean ambitions would inevitably mean conflict with Britain and France, and therefore he needed the Axis. However, when, on 14 March 1939 Hitler overthrew the Munich agreement and occupied Prague, Mussolini was shocked.

Key question
Was Mussolini really the peacemaker in 1938?

Key dates
Munich Conference: 29 September 1938

Hitler marched into Prague: 14–15 March 1939

Albania

By this stage Ciano, Italy's foreign minister, had become anti-Nazi and was opposed to closer relations, but Mussolini continued to feel that only Germany could help him to secure his Mediterranean claims, although exactly what they were was not clear. His speeches would refer to Corsica, Tunisia, Malta, Cyprus, and even Greece, Turkey and Egypt. Mussolini was jealous of Hitler's success and Ciano had little difficulty in persuading him that it would be a good idea to take over Albania, a country that Italy had dominated economically for many years. The move was designed to defuse discontent at home and match the Germans, indeed the move was almost anti-German as it seemed to assert Italian claims to the Balkans. However, Hitler did not object and it made Mussolini more inclined to accept the German offer of a military alliance, especially since Chamberlain had subsequently, on 13 April, offered guarantees to Greece which seemed to thwart Italian ambitions in the Balkans. On 22 May Ciano was dispatched to sign a deal with the Germans.

Key question
Why did Mussolini invade Albania?

Key dates
Italy seized Albania: 7 April 1939

Pact of Steel signed: 22 May 1939

Pact of Steel 1939

So, by May 1939 the Axis became the Pact of Steel, a full-blown military alliance, which was designed to ensure that each would assist the other in the event of war. Mussolini wanted a key provision that there should be no European war for 3 years (until 1942), but the Germans drew up the final text and made no mention of this. Neither Ciano nor Mussolini read the small print and were later disturbed to discover the omission. Hitler had no intention of waiting 3 years. Whereas the day after the pact was signed Hitler was preparing for war, Mussolini was already trying

Key question
Why did Mussolini finally agree to a full military alliance?

Key date

Nazi–Soviet Pact:
23 August 1939

to wriggle out of the commitment. He offered Hitler advice;
Hitler did not reply. He suggested a conference about Danzig and
Poland, but Hitler did not want a conference.

On 11 August Ciano went to Salzburg, where Ribbentrop
(foreign minister since February) told him of Hitler's plans to
invade Poland. Mussolini and Ciano realised that this meant a
European war: they were both horrified. Then, on 23 August,
Hitler confounded the world by doing a deal with Stalin – the
Nazi–Soviet Pact (see page 132). For Mussolini this was both a
shock and a godsend: *Il Duce* could not possibly agree to be on
the same side as the Bolsheviks. He immediately told Hitler he
would be unable to fulfil his military obligations, but cited a lack
of *matériel*. Hitler surprised him by asking exactly what he
needed, so the Italian High Command drew up a ludicrously long
list for 40,000 trainloads of equipment! Hitler accepted
Mussolini's position and released him from his obligations. Now
he could stay out. Hitler, of course, did not need Mussolini and in
any event felt that his startling diplomatic coup with the Soviets
would render the democracies impotent: in fact he thought he
had avoided a general war. Nevertheless, he warned Mussolini –
and this would turn out to be quite prescient – that the two
regimes were interlocked, and that the fate of Fascist Italy very
much depended on the fortunes of Nazi Germany.

Non-belligerence

Key question
Why did Mussolini
stay out of the war in
1939 and then
change his mind in
1940?

When a general war did break out in September 1939 Mussolini
felt ashamed that he was not part of it. He craved military glory
and felt that neutrality – or **non-belligerence** as he called it in an
effort to disguise what it really was – tarnished his image.
Moreover, he was well aware that Italy had let Germany down
before in 1914. These concerns did not worry the Italian people
who were delighted at the outcome; neutrality was very popular.

War

Key dates

Germany invaded
Poland: 1 September
1939

Britain and France
declared war on
Germany:
3 September 1939

Mussolini declared
war on Britain and
France: 10 June 1940

In March 1940 Ribbentrop came to Rome to explain that Hitler
was about to attack in the west; the message was Italy should join
or remain 'a European state of modest claims'. A week later
Mussolini met Hitler at Brenner and agreed to join when he
could, but was still playing for time. However, after 10 May when
the Germans swept through the Netherlands, Belgium and
northern France in a lightning attack, he knew he could delay
no longer. On 10 June, in a move President Roosevelt described
as a 'stab in the back', Mussolini declared war on Britain and
France. With France about to fall and Britain's position looking
quite hopeless, this did not seem to be a foolish decision at the
time. Indeed, it was even quite popular with some of the Italian
people as it looked like an opportunity too good to miss. No one
at this stage envisaged defeat, unconditional surrender and
civil war.

Key term

Non-belligerence
Literally, not
waging war.

Summary diagram: From Axis to alliance 1936–9

| 1936: The Spanish Civil War cements Italo–German relations |
| 1936: The Axis |
| 1938: The Axis allows the *Anschluss* to occur |
| 1939: Mussolini agrees to the Pact of Steel |
| 1940: The Pact of Steel eventually leads to war |

4 | Conclusion 1933–9

The real turning point?

There is no doubt that to some extent Hitler modelled his movement on Mussolini's and he clearly admired the man, but, as we have seen, this admiration was initially not reciprocated, and the status of Austria proved to be an obstacle to good relations. Yet Mussolini did see some advantage in playing off Germany against Britain and France in order to further Italian interests. However, this policy brought few concrete benefits and so *Il Duce* decided to take the initiative.

Thus, the real turning point in European relations in this period was the Italian invasion of Abyssinia in 1935. This put the final nail in the coffin of the League of Nations and virtually destroyed Italy's relationship with the Western democracies of Britain and France. Public opinion in these countries was appalled by Italian atrocities and Mussolini for his part was angered by British and French opposition. Abyssinia brought out a basic convergence of interest between Fascist Italy and Nazi Germany. They were both expansionist and revisionist in terms of the 1919 settlement, and hostile to the chief beneficiaries of that settlement which stood in the way of their expansionist goals (i.e. Britain and France).

A common ideology?

Mussolini recognised that only Germany would back the challenge to Anglo-French hegemony in the Mediterranean. For Hitler, Italy could occupy Britain and France while he concentrated on the East. The Axis met the interests of both countries. But if the Axis was sustained by common interests it was also sustained by common ideology. The meeting of interests and ideology can be best seen in the Spanish Civil War, where a right-wing military dictator was aided to oust a democratically elected government.

Key question
What was the real turning point in European relations during the years 1933–9?

Italy's Mediterranean ambitions

If Abyssinia had led to a break with the democracies, then the Spanish Civil War led to the formation (and continuation) of the Axis. Now Mussolini sacrificed Austria to Hitler and finally committed himself to a military alliance – without even reading the treaty! There was, however, a logic in allying himself with the strongest power. A few months before signing the Pact of Steel, the Italian dictator had made an important speech in which he portrayed Italy as a prisoner in its own sea, the Mediterranean, the bars of the prison being Corsica, Tunisia (French) and Malta and Cyprus (British), the prison guards being Gibraltar (British) and the Suez Canal (British and French). Only with German help could his ambitions to dominate the Mediterranean be realised.

Hitler, the real beneficiary

In truth, the real beneficiary of Mussolini's diplomatic revolution was of course, Adolf Hitler. He was able to use the cover of Abyssinia to reoccupy the Rhineland; he was able to use the Spanish Civil War to bring Mussolini closer to him; and he was thereby able to occupy Austria with Italy's acquiescence. Thereafter, he was able to force the pace. It was, after all, a very unequal relationship, reflecting the two countries' relative economic and military strength: Germany was strong, Italy was weak. Conquering Abyssinia and aiding the ungrateful Franco had crippled Italian finances. In fact, from the German point of view Italy had largely served its purpose between the years 1936 and 1938 and thereafter became something of a liability, although Hitler remained true to his word and never abandoned *Il Duce*. It is difficult to see what Italy got out of the relationship. In June 1940 it must have looked as though the logic of Mussolini's policy was about to pay off, but it did not; instead it lead to defeat, death and destruction.

Study Guide: Advanced-level Questions

In the style of Edexcel

In the paper you are given an hour to write a single essay for which 60 marks are awarded. There will be a choice of two questions. Here are three relevant to the chapter you have just read.

(a) What key factors explain Germany's changing relations with Italy in these years?

Source: Edexcel, June 2002

(b) How far was shared ideology responsible for improved relations between Italy and Germany in the years 1936–9?

Source: Edexcel, June 2003

(c) How important was the Spanish Civil War in turning Italy and Germany into diplomatic partners over the period 1933–9?

Source: Edexcel, January 2004

Exam tips

The cross-references are intended to take you straight to the material that will help you to answer the questions.

See Chapter 2 (page 47) for some general advice on essay-writing skills.

(a) Obviously this question requires you to trawl through the entire period; however, you must be careful not to get bogged down in a simple narrative of events. To be analytical you need to identify the key factors with some justification and evaluate their relative importance; for example, Hitler's initial enthusiasm for a relationship was frustrated both by Mussolini's coolness and by the assassination of Dollfuss (page 50).

The key factors in the change in relationship are obviously:

- Abyssinia and Mussolini's dissatisfaction with the democracies (an ongoing factor tied to his Mediterranean ambitions; pages 52–6)
- joint support for Franco in the Spanish Civil War (pages 57–9)
- ideological affinity (pages 50, 57–8 and 66)
- the development of a personal relationship (pages 61 and 63)
- reach a reasoned judgement based on an evaluation of all these factors – are they all equally important (this judgement would be unusual and is usually the refuge of the lazy intellect) or can you create a hierarchy of importance?

(b) This question is similar to the first except that it directs you to consider one key factor:

- Shared ideology, which you have to discuss in some detail even if you consider it to be of little importance (pages 50, 57–8 and 66).
- You then have to measure its importance against other factors: such as Abyssinia (page 52), relations with Britain and France (pages 53–6), and the Spanish Civil War (pages 57–9).
- Reach a reasoned judgement.

(c) This question, like the second, directs you to consider one factor – the Spanish Civil War – which you would have to evaluate against all the other factors.

Although questions **(b)** and **(c)** require you to call on the same range of causal factors, roughly a quarter to a third of the answer needs to be devoted to the main factor stated in the question.

4

Hitler Changes Gear 1937–8

POINTS TO CONSIDER

This chapter steps back a few years from the end of the previous chapter and will look at Hitler's planning and opportunism. The key areas examined are:

- The Hossbach Memorandum, November 1937
- The *Anschluss* with Austria, March 1938
- The Munich Conference, September 1938
- Conclusion 1937–8

What you have to decide is how far Hitler was in control of events and how far he was reacting to them.

Key dates

1937	November 5	Hossbach Memorandum
1938	March 12	German occupation of Austria
	September 15	Chamberlain visited Hitler at Berchtesgaden
	September 22	Chamberlain met Hitler for the second time at Bad Godesberg
	September 29	Munich Conference

Key question
Can the Hossbach Memorandum be taken seriously?

1 | The Hossbach Memorandum, November 1937

Background

By the autumn of 1937 Hitler appears to have concluded that time was not on Germany's side and that it must go on to the offensive sooner rather than later. The problem was that, by embarking on a massive rearmament programme, Germany had started an arms race. Moreover, because of Germany's limited resources in comparison with its rivals such as Russia, it was a race it was bound to lose if it went on for any length of time. Yet while Germany was ahead there was a 'window of opportunity' that Hitler could exploit prior to the other powers catching up. He therefore felt a growing pressure to act quickly, using Germany's temporary superiority to expand its resources by plundering its neighbours.

Despite Hitler's concerns about rivals' rearmament, a glance at Table 4.1 will show that German military strength had developed at a remarkable rate; by the end of 1937 Germany had become

Table 4.1: Percentage of GNP devoted to defence

	Germany	Britain
1933	1.0	3.0
1934	3.0	3.0
1935	7.4	3.3
1936	12.4	4.2
1937	11.8	5.6
1938	16.6	8.1
1939	23.0	21.4

the strongest military power in Europe. The rise of Germany was matched by the decline of France. France's weakness and passivity were the result of internal problems and unstable governments, and, from its point of view, of British policy. The fiasco of sanctions against Italy (see page 54) had lost France a friend and made it even more reliant on the British, who were themselves unreliable. The Rhineland episode (see page 36), when Hitler marched his army into the demilitarised zone unopposed, 'marked both a strategic and psychological surrender by France' (Bell). Meanwhile, Britain continued to pursue the illusion of a general European settlement, a renegotiation of Locarno, but this was a complete non-starter. Thus by the end of 1937 the balance of power had swung decisively away from Britain and France to Germany and Italy. Italy, of course, was something of a **paper tiger**, but Germany was not; and Germany now held the initiative.

The meeting

Accordingly Hitler began to take the initiative. Already in the summer of 1937, Field Marshal von Blomberg had drawn up a directive concerning 'preparations of the armed forces for a possible war' that had, among other things, discussed moves against Czechoslovakia and Austria. Then, on 5 November 1937, Hitler had a 4-hour meeting with five of his **top brass**, in which he was a little more specific about his thoughts for the future. Colonel Friedrich Hossbach, his military **adjutant**, took notes and 5 days later wrote up a secret memorandum based on the notes and his memory. This document took on some significance later at the Nuremberg trials, although all that exists is a copy of a copy. Indeed, it has been the subject of a great deal of historical controversy ever since. Was it a statement of intent or a mere exploration of possibilities?

THOSE PRESENT AT THE MEETING				
		Hitler		
von Fritsch (Army)	Raeder (Navy)	Göring (Air force)	von Blomberg (War Minister)	von Neurath (Foreign Minister)
		Hossbach		

Reasons for the meeting

The meeting occurred as a response to Admiral Raeder's complaints about cuts and postponements in the naval programme. The objective of the meeting was to resolve the conflict over priorities in the allocation of raw materials and labour. Hitler took the opportunity to make an often rambling and wide-ranging speech, as Hossbach records:

His exposition was to follow the fruit of thorough deliberation and the experiences of his four and a half years of power. He wished to

Key question
What changes to German foreign policy did Hitler propose at this meeting?

explain to the gentlemen present the basic ideas concerning the opportunities for the development of our position in the field of foreign affairs and its requirements, and he asked, in the interest of a long-term German policy, that his exposition be regarded, in the event of his death, as his last will and testament.

The *Führer* then continued: The aim of German policy was to make secure and to preserve the racial community and to enlarge it. It was therefore a question of space.

Hitler then went on to identify Germany's two main enemies, Britain and France, and he reached the conclusion that 'Germany's problem could be solved only by the use of force'. He then posed three **contingencies**. The first was that the rearmament rate of the other powers meant that time was not on Germany's side; hence 'it was his unalterable determination to solve Germany's problem of space by 1943–5 at the latest'. Prior to 1943–5, in contingencies two and three, Hitler felt that if France was embroiled in either internal strife or war then Germany could act sooner 'to overthrow Czechoslovakia and Austria simultaneously'.

Key term

Contingency
Something that may happen.

Consequences of the meeting

Key question
What concrete measures were taken as a result of the November 1937 meeting?

Operation Green
First of all, Operation Green (the attack on Czechoslovakia) was radically altered. At the time of the meeting it was envisaged as a defensive measure because the Czechs were allied to France: it was designed to prevent a two-front war. A month later General Jodl, Chief of Operations, gave the plan a more aggressive slant:

When Germany has achieved complete preparedness for war in all spheres, then the military conditions will have been created for carrying out an offensive war against Czechoslovakia, so that the solution of the German problem of living space can be carried to a victorious conclusion even if one or another of the Great Powers intervene against us. … Should the political situation not develop, the execution of 'Operation Green' from our side will have to be postponed for years. If, however, a situation arises which, owing to Britain's aversion to a general European war, through her lack of interest in the Central European problem and because of a conflict breaking out between Italy and France in the Mediterranean, creates the probability that Germany will face no other opponent than Russia on Czechoslovakia's side, then 'Operation Green' will start before the completion of Germany's full preparedness for war.

A purge?
Secondly, in the ensuing discussion after Hitler's speech, both von Blomberg and von Fritsch voiced their objections. Subsequently, both men were removed (in February 1938), but this may be mere coincidence. Hitler had not been planning major changes in the government or military; indeed he attended Blomberg's wedding in January. However, Blomberg was made to resign when it was discovered that his new wife had been a prostitute; and von

Fritsch, a single man, was set up by Himmler and Göring and falsely accused of homosexual practices. Von Neurath, who had expressed reservations after the meeting, in January, was also removed from office at the same time.

Blomberg's position as Minister of War was abolished and the **OKW** put in its place. Hitler himself took on the office of Commander-in-Chief of the Armed Forces (also held by Blomberg) in addition to the post of Supreme Commander which he already held, and he made Keitel his Chief of Staff; von Brauchitsch, a 'yes man', replaced von Fritsch as army commander, and von Ribbentrop replaced von Neurath at the Foreign Office. In addition, 14 senior generals were retired, 46 others reassigned, and new ambassadors were appointed to the key cities of Rome, Tokyo and Vienna.

A final consequence of the meeting was that Hitler made it clear that he had finally abandoned any thought of *rapprochement* with Britain.

Conclusion

Of course, those who criticise the Hossbach Memorandum point out that the *Anschluss* owed little to planning and that there was no war with Czechoslovakia. They also point out that there was no mention of the invasions of Poland or Russia. All these criticisms are valid. Still, the Hossbach Memorandum remains important when taken in conjunction with other evidence, for instance, General Beck's (Head of General Staff) point-by-point comments on its content written on 12 November and Jodl's revisions of 7 December, already quoted on the previous page.

It was clearly taken seriously at the time and led to practical results. It also demonstrated beyond doubt Hitler's warlike expansionist intentions and reflected his growing sense of urgency (probably prompted by a bout of ill health at the time). And his comment that 'Britain, almost certainly, and probably France as well, had written off the Czechs and were reconciled to the fact that the question for Germany would be cleared up in due course', turned out to be remarkably accurate. However, as well as reflecting urgency and expansionism, the talk does suggest, by its various contingencies, that Hitler was trying to anticipate a wide variety of scenarios so that he could take advantage of the situation when any opportunity arose.

However, of more significance, perhaps, were the changes in personnel in February 1938 that made it much more likely that Hitler would be able to get his own way in the future without any objection from the army or the foreign ministry. As has been indicated, the purge of the traditional élites was in all probability an improvisation, but the Hossbach meeting did highlight their opposition. Characteristically, Hitler responded 'by seizing the opportunity and, with a typically daring forward move' turned an embarrassment into a bloodless purge. 'Following the *Reichstag* Fire and the **Röhm Crisis**, the Blomberg–Fritsch affair was the third great milestone on the way to *Führer* absolutist power' (Kershaw). The army, the one institution of state that could still

Key terms

OKW
Oberkommando der Wermacht: High Command of the Armed Forces.

Röhm Crisis
This refers to the 'Night of the Long Knives', 30 June 1934, when Hitler eliminated Ernst Röhm, a potential rival and leader of the SA.

Key question
What criticisms can be levelled at the memorandum?

topple him, was emasculated and Hitler was increasingly surrounded by those who would simply agree with him and do his bidding. So, his visionary intentions were able to come to replace practical, rational policy objectives. In short, he was in a much better position to take the decisions he wanted to take.

The key debate

Some historians see the Hossbach Memorandum as a significant turning point in Hitler's foreign policy. Noakes and Pridham stated in 1988: 'In this address Hitler had for the first time expressed a concrete commitment to war in terms of specific goals – *Anschluss* with Austria and the destruction of Czechoslovakia – and within a specific time limit – 1943–5.' However, A.J.P. Taylor, in the first edition of his book, *The Origins of the Second World War*, stated that, 'Hitler's exposition was in large part day-dreaming, unrelated to what followed in real life', and he further stated in 1965 that the meeting 'had no significance'. Taylor attacked the source itself, pointing out that it was not a proper record, and that it was not signed by Hitler. However, others at the conference agreed after the war that Hossbach's account was a pretty reliable record of what was said. Moreover, the real significance of the meeting lay in its consequences: Hitler's remarks were taken seriously.

Some key books in the debate
P.M.H. Bell, *The Origins of the Second World War in Europe* (Longman, 1997).
J. Noakes and G. Pridham, *Nazism 1919–1945, Vol. 3, Foreign Policy, War and Racial Extermination. A Documentary Reader* (University of Exeter, 1988).
A.J.P. Taylor, *Origins of the Second World War* (Hamish Hamilton, 1961).

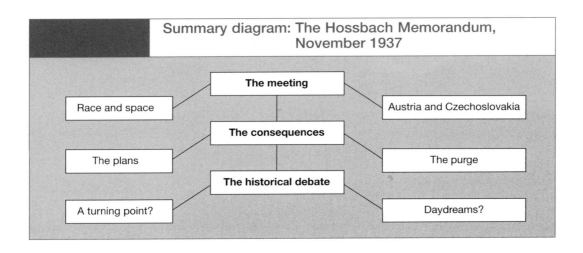

Summary diagram: The Hossbach Memorandum, November 1937

2 | The *Anschluss* with Austria, March 1938

Context

Since the abortive *putsch* of 1934 (see page 34), Hitler had been cautious towards Austria, the more so from 1936 as he did not want to jeopardise the growing friendship with Italy (see page 57). During 1937 it was Göring who increasingly took the initiative over Austria, but he envisaged *Anschluss* as evolutionary and peaceful. During Mussolini's visit in September 1937, Göring took *Il Duce*'s ambiguity on the subject as a green light – a position reinforced by a report from von Ribbentrop on 6 November: Mussolini had told him that he accepted that Austria was a German country. Without Italian support, Austria had little chance of sustaining independence. Moreover, Austria could expect little support from Britain either. When Lord Halifax visited Germany on 19 November 1937, he stated that certain changes in Eastern Europe, notably with regard to Austria, Czechoslovakia and Danzig, 'could probably not be avoided in the long run'. Accordingly, Hitler was convinced that Britain would not intervene, and when Halifax subsequently became Foreign Secretary in February 1938, this only served to reinforce his view.

Schuschnigg forced to make concessions

The opportunity to intervene in Austria arose early in 1938 and was precipitated by the destabilising activities of the Austrian Nazis and Austrian Chancellor Schuschnigg's exasperation with them. Schuschnigg came to Berchtesgaden on 12 February 1938 to discuss the matter with Hitler and there followed a remarkable meeting. Over the course of the day Hitler ranted and raved and subjected the Austrian Chancellor to a barrage of verbal assaults, psychological pressure and threats of invasion. This was a most unusual way to conduct business between two heads of state, but it worked. Schuschnigg was forced to accept 10 demands including the appointment of an Austrian Nazi, Seyss-Inquart, in the politically important post of **Interior Minister**, demands that would make Austria into a virtual **satellite** of Germany. Indeed, on 26 February Hitler said as much to some leading Austrian Nazis when he told them to drop the revolutionary approach as it was unnecessary. But then the situation changed.

Plebiscite

The Austrian Nazis continued to hold threatening demonstrations and Seyss-Inquart increasingly came to dominate the government. Accordingly, Schuschnigg tried to retrieve the situation by a desperate move: on 9 March he announced a plebiscite for 13 March on whether or not the Austrian people wanted 'a free and German, an independent and social, a Christian and united Austria'. This was a bold move and it looked as though Hitler might lose; most Austrians were pro-German, but ambivalent about union because it meant Nazism.

Key question
Did Hitler plan the *Anschluss* or was it an improvisation?

Key terms

Putsch
A violent uprising.

Interior Minister
Minister responsible for internal security with control of the police.

Satellite
In this case, a small country nominally independent, but controlled by or dependent on another.

David Low's cartoon published in the London *Evening Standard* in 1938 commenting on the *Anschluss*.

Hitler was stunned. Göring effectively took charge of events and argued for military intervention, but there were no plans; however, the army quickly and willingly drew some up. In the event they were not needed as the matter was all settled on 11 March by telephone calls and telegrams. Hitler immediately wrote to Mussolini justifying German intervention and was relieved to receive a telephone call from Prince Philip of Hesse in which he informed Hitler that the Italian leader had raised no objections to the *Anschluss* (for the text see page 63). Schuschnigg, on the other hand, could get no reply from *Il Duce*, who would not pick up the phone. He could not get any joy from London either, where it was felt that *Anschluss* was inevitable and desired by the majority. France, not unusually, was paralysed by a ministerial crisis. Schuschnigg, therefore, postponed the plebiscite and resigned.

Occupation

On 12 March the German army marched in, but it was more of a parade than an invasion. Remarkably just as no plans had been made for the takeover, so too no plans had been laid for the actual implementation of the union: Hitler seems to have made this decision on the spur of the moment on 13 March during an emotional visit to the Austrian town of Linz, where he had grown up. So, Austria was annexed and became a province of the Reich, a fact which was subsequently confirmed by an all too predictable 99 per cent of the vote in a plebiscite.

Key date

German occupation of Austria: 12 March 1938

An improvisation

Anschluss with Austria was a great triumph for Hitler and enormously enhanced his personal prestige (as well as adding 295 million *Reichmarks* to the treasury). Moreover, 'the danger of a European war arising out of the Austrian crisis was almost nil' (Bell). However, the British backbench Conservative MP Winston Churchill stated in the House of Commons on 14 March: 'Europe is confronted with a programme of aggression, nicely calculated and timed, unfolding stage by stage', but in this case Churchill was wrong. What is important to remember about this crisis is that the date and method of *Anschluss* were forced on Hitler by circumstances, and were *not* part of a pre-arranged plan. Hitler was compelled to improvise.

But if *Anschluss* itself was not part of a plan, it was certainly another step on the road to war. The manner of the union created unease. Moreover, on 24 March 1938, Neville Chamberlain, the British Prime Minister since May 1937, warned of the dangers of a war starting in Europe. Overnight Czechoslovakia had been made more vulnerable as it was now bordered by German territory to the north, west and south, and Hitler's self-confidence had reached new heights: Czechoslovakia would be his next objective.

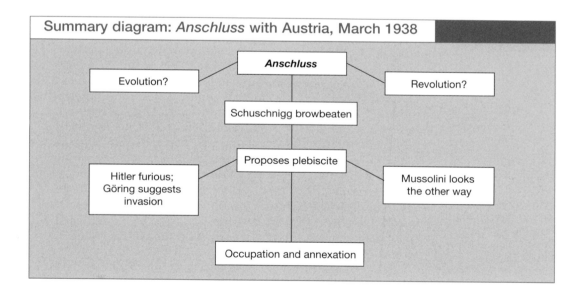

Summary diagram: *Anschluss* with Austria, March 1938

3 | The Munich Conference, September 1938

Context

Hitler despised the Czechs as 'sub-people': he possessed a personal animosity toward them that was probably the result of his contact with a few individuals in Vienna in his youth. He wished to destroy their state, but that would not be easy: the Czechs had a powerful army, a vibrant arms industry and good

Key question
To what extent did Hitler take an evolutionary approach to the 'Czech problem'?

Key terms

Sudetenland
An area in the north-west part of Czechoslovakia that contained Czech border defences and which, as part of the Austro-Hungarian Empire prior to 1919, had never been part of Germany.

Evolutionary approach
Referring to Hitler being prepared to take a slow approach in the belief that over time events would develop in his favour.

border fortifications. Moreover, they had a military alliance with France, prompting Hitler to describe the country as 'a French aircraft carrier in the middle of Europe'. Therefore, the *Führer* sought to undermine the state by exploiting its complex ethnic structure; in particular, by supporting the aspirations of the 3.5 million Germans who lived there (mainly in the **Sudetenland**; see the map overleaf).

Hitler had been funding the Sudeten German Party since 1935, but there was a limit to what internal destabilisation could achieve. Czechoslovakia was an international diplomatic issue, but unbeknown to Hitler both Britain and France concluded in March 1938 that there was little they could do to assist directly in Czech defence. However, at this stage the German leader's approach was **evolutionary**. When on 28 March he summoned Henlein, the leader of the Sudeten Nazi Party, he simply stated that he would settle the problem in the 'not-too-distant future', but beyond that he would not be drawn. Nevertheless, Henlein was encouraged to continue his subversive tactics, negotiate demands and constantly raise them. On 24 April Henlein did just that when he presented the Czech government with his Eight Demands, which consisted of autonomy and various special rights for the German minority.

Yet a document of 20 May makes it quite clear that Hitler was in no hurry to solve the Czech problem. In an interim draft of Operation Green, Hitler told his generals:

> It is not my intention to smash Czechoslovakia by military action in the immediate future without provocation, unless an unavoidable development of the political conditions within Czechoslovakia forces the issue, or political events in Europe create a particularly favourable opportunity which may perhaps never recur.

Of course, this was not in any way a moderate document and it spells out Hitler's commitment to opportunism, but it certainly goes against the idea that he had a strict timetable.

May Crisis

Key question
How did the May Crisis transform the situation?

Ironically, on the very same day a crisis erupted – the so-called May Crisis – which made Hitler change his mind completely. On 20 May, acting on (unfounded) rumours of German troop movements, President Beneš of Czechoslovakia ordered a partial mobilisation of the Czech army and called on the Western powers to intervene. The new French government took a firm line, as did Britain: although the Czech issue was not a vital interest, the British did not wish to see a unilateral solution imposed on the Czechs by German military force. Accordingly, both governments warned Hitler. Hitler made a denial (because the rumours were unfounded), but was infuriated that he had appeared to yield to Anglo-French pressure. He felt that he had been made to look foolish.

The partitioning of Czechoslovakia 1938.

Consequences

Accordingly, in a fit of pique, on 28 May Hitler summoned a meeting of leading advisers and generals. Fritz Wiedemann (Hitler's adjutant) recalled Hitler informing them:

> 'I am utterly determined that Czechoslovakia should disappear from the map.' He turned to the generals and stated: 'Right, we will deal with the situation in the East [i.e. Czechoslovakia] first. Then I shall give you 3 or 4 years and then we will sort things out in the West [i.e. France and Britain].'
>
> Two days later he issued a new order for Operation Green: 'It is my unalterable decision to smash Czechoslovakia by military action in the near future. It is the business of the political leadership to await or bring about the suitable moment from a political or military point of view.'

A covering letter from Keitel stated that the execution of the plan 'must be assured by 1 October 1938 at the latest'. So it appears that an attack of hurt pride produced the crisis, a view supported by an entry in the diary of von Weizäcker, the State Secretary in the Foreign Ministry, when he later summed up the crisis: 'His [Hitler's] resentment, stemming from 22 May when the English accused him of pulling back, led him on to the path of war'.

Another important consequence of the May Crisis was that the Western democracies had also been disturbed by the whole incident, but their reaction was pacific. They felt that they had been taken to the brink of war and came to believe (and resent the fact) that the crisis had been manufactured by the Czechs. Neville Chamberlain, in particular, was now determined to achieve a negotiated solution to this problem which could only be favourable to Germany.

Chamberlain's three visits

Berchtesgaden

Tension mounted throughout the summer of 1938. A barrage of anti-Czech propaganda was put out by the Germans which unnerved the democracies. German troop movements by now were quite genuine. The crisis reached a climax at the beginning of September, when on the 5th, President Beneš granted the Sudeten Germans virtual **autonomy** in an effort to defuse the situation. But Hitler wanted his war and Henlein was told to ignore this offer; Hitler used the arrest of two Sudeten deputies as an excuse to break off negotiations. He followed this up on 12 September with a violent speech at the Nuremberg Rally threatening war. This was followed by riots in the Sudetenland which now convinced Chamberlain that war was imminent.

The British Prime Minister at once resolved to take his first aeroplane journey and flew to see Hitler at Berchtesgaden on 15 September where he agreed to Hitler's terms, subject to consultation. Hitler was none too pleased, but felt that this rather ridiculous figure (as he described him) would not be back. In the meantime he contacted the Polish and Hungarian governments

Key question
Why did it take three visits to achieve a settlement?

Key date
Chamberlain visited Hitler at Berchtesgaden: 15 September 1938

Key term
Autonomy
The right of self-government.

(both of which had claims on Czech territory) and stirred up the Slovaks (who resented Czech domination).

Bad Godesberg

Chamberlain obtained French acceptance for the **cession** of the Sudetenland to Germany on 18 September and the reluctant agreement of the Czechs on 21 September. However, when he flew back to see Hitler, this time at Bad Godesberg, he was amazed and dismayed to discover that the German leader had raised the stakes. Hitler now wanted a more rapid hand-over and a settlement of Polish and Hungarian territorial claims on the Czech state (see the map on page 78). The meeting broke up with no agreement and it now looked like war.

Key date

Chamberlain met Hitler for the second time in Bad Godesberg: 22 September 1938

Key terms

Cession
The giving up of rights, property, territory, etc.

Rump Czech state
The small Czech state – or 'rump' – left over after partition.

Munich

However, a week later, assailed by last-minute doubts, Hitler pulled back from the brink. Why? There would appear to be a number of reasons:

- On 20 September the French began mobilisation.
- On 28 September the British mobilised their fleet.
- It was now clear the democracies were not bluffing.
- The Czechs too were ready to fight.
- In addition, Hitler's generals took fright and (rightly) maintained that Germany was not ready for a major war.
- Hitler also noted the lack of enthusiasm displayed by the ordinary German people and he was influenced by Göring, who was totally opposed to war at this stage and advised caution.
- The opportunity to step back from the brink was conveniently provided by Mussolini, who proposed to act as a mediator at a Four Power Conference (although in truth his plan was drawn up by the German Foreign Office! – see page 64).

So, on 28 September Hitler agreed to a conference in Munich to be attended by Chamberlain, Daladier for France and Mussolini (the Czechs and the Soviets were not invited, despite the fact that the former had a military alliance with the latter). There was relief throughout Europe, not least in Germany.

The Munich Agreement

The meeting took place on 29 September and in the early hours of the 30th it was agreed that:

Key date

Munich Conference: 29 September 1938

- The Sudetenland was to be occupied by Germany between 1 and 10 October.
- Polish and Hungarian claims were to be settled.
- An international commission was to determine the final frontier.
- A four-power guarantee was to protect the territorial integrity of the **rump Czech state**.

Of greater importance to Chamberlain, however, was the subsequent Anglo-German Declaration; this was the piece of

Chamberlain returns in triumph. This photograph shows the British Prime Minister's arrival at Heston Aerodrome near London in September 1938.

paper that he proudly held up at Heston Aerodrome on his return. It stated:

We, the German *Führer* and Chancellor and the British Prime Minister, have had a further meeting today and are agreed in recognising that the question of Anglo-German relations is of the first importance for the two countries and for Europe.

We regard the agreement signed last night and the Anglo-German Naval Agreement as symbolic of the desire of our two peoples never to go to war with one another again.

We are resolved that the method of consultation shall be the method adopted to deal with any other questions that may concern our two countries, and we are determined to continue our efforts to remove possible sources of difference and thus contribute to assure the peace of Europe.

Chamberlain famously stated that this was 'peace for our time'. 'In reality, it was peace for a time' (Crozier). For Hitler it was just a piece of paper that could easily be torn up.

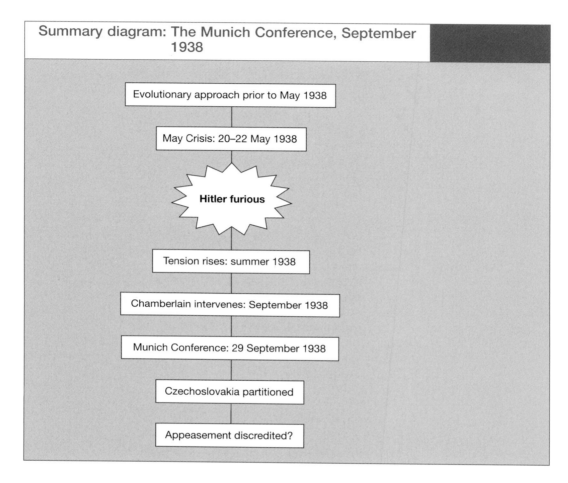

Summary diagram: The Munich Conference, September 1938

Evolutionary approach prior to May 1938

May Crisis: 20–22 May 1938

Hitler furious

Tension rises: summer 1938

Chamberlain intervenes: September 1938

Munich Conference: 29 September 1938

Czechoslovakia partitioned

Appeasement discredited?

4 | Conclusion 1937–8

Key question
Was Hitler a planner or an opportunist?

Hitler felt cheated of his military victory: 'That fellow Chamberlain has spoiled my entry into Prague', he was overheard to remark. And it has been rightly pointed out that 'a general war was averted in 1938 not, as is so often asserted, because Chamberlain cravenly gave way to Hitler, but because Hitler gave way to the western powers' (Overy). However, Hitler was not going to back down next time and on 21 October he issued a directive for the 'liquidation of the remainder of the Czech state'. So much for the four-power guarantee. Indeed, by avoiding a war over Czechoslovakia, both Germany and the Western powers probably made war more certain next time.

The year 1938 had been a very good one for Hitler, but his successes were to some extent the result of fortuitous circumstances and the acquiescence of others. However, for Britain and France, Munich turned out to be the limit of

Key term

Apogee
The highest point.

concession; it was the **apogee** of appeasement, but it was also to be its mortal wound. Chamberlain felt that the sacrifice of the Czechs was a necessary price to pay for peace. Others were not so sure. Churchill declared: 'we have sustained a total and unmitigated defeat'. Attlee, the Labour Party leader, concurred:

> The events of the last few days constitute one of the greatest diplomatic defeats that this country and France have ever sustained. There can be no doubt that it is a tremendous victory for Herr Hitler. Without firing a shot, by the mere display of military force, he has achieved a dominating position in Europe which Germany failed to win after four years of war ... He has destroyed the last fortress of democracy in eastern Europe that stood in the way of his ambition. He has opened the way for the food, the oil, and the resources that he requires in order to consolidate his military power, and he has successfully defeated and reduced to impotence the forces that might have stood against the rule of violence. The cause [of the crisis] was not the existence of minorities in Czechoslovakia; it was not that the position of the Sudeten Germans had become intolerable. It was not the wonderful principle of self-determination. It was because Herr Hitler had decided that the time was ripe for another step forward in his design to dominate Europe. ... Hitler has successfully asserted the law of the jungle.

These voices were as yet in a minority, but they were growing in number as many came to feel uncomfortable about the shabby treatment of the Czechs and giving in to Hitler. Munich did not stop Chamberlain from continuing to attempt appeasement, but for the majority it proved to be a turning point. For an analysis of appeasement in particular and the policies of the democracies in general, you are advised to turn to the next chapter, but before you do it might be worth taking another look at Hitler's successes in 1938 to see how they fit in to the debate about planning and opportunism that we referred to in the opening chapter.

Improvisation?

As we have seen, Hitler was forced to improvise when he took over Austria. There was no plan ready and precious little preparation (General Jodl reported that 70 per cent of the trucks broke down *en route*!). He was pushed into *Anschluss* by Schuschnigg's threat of a plebiscite. Similarly, over Czechoslovakia there were no immediate plans for a takeover; Hitler favoured the evolutionary approach but he abandoned this in May 1938 in the wake of what he felt to be a humiliation. Jodl recorded in his diary that Hitler felt 'a loss of prestige ... which he was no longer willing to take'. So he planned a war. But then he did not go to war. Instead of the destruction of Czechoslovakia, he settled for a partial partition.

So, Hitler had no plan for *Anschluss*, but annexed Austria, and he had a plan for a war with Czechoslovakia, but he did not implement it. What does this tell us? It tells us that Hitler could improvise, be flexible, be an opportunist; it tells us he could change his mind. Does that then mean he was not a planner? The majority of historians, including his latest biographer Ian Kershaw, say no. There seems to be no doubt that the absorption of both Austria and Czechoslovakia were long-term objectives of Hitler's and, as we have seen, they were referred to in the Hossbach Memorandum. After all, Hitler was only 'forced into' the takeover of Austria because taking over Austria was something that he wanted to do: otherwise he could have simply left that country alone. And his subsequent action in occupying Prague in March 1939 (see page 124) confirmed that he also wanted to expand into Czechoslovakia. So, he had objectives, but the circumstances of fulfilling them were often not of his own making.

Objectives

Let us remind ourselves, at the risk of repetition, what Hitler's main objectives were: he wished to overthrow the Versailles Treaty, unite all Germans, expel all Jews and win *lebensraum* in the East (although quite why Hitler did not refer to the conquest of the Soviet Union and destruction of Bolshevism in the Hossbach Memorandum remains an unanswerable puzzle). However, within the broad framework of these long-term objectives Hitler was prepared to improvise and be opportunistic, as indeed he was in 1938. To some extent this diagnosis of his approach was confirmed by Hitler himself in a secret speech about the previous year to a large number of senior officers on 10 February 1939; although admittedly he wished to emphasise his forethought rather than any improvisation:

> There was no doubt that these questions [i.e. Austria and Czechoslovakia] would have to be solved and so all these decisions were not ideas which were realised at the moment of their conception, but were long-made plans which I was determined to realise the moment I thought the circumstances at the time would be favourable.

Hitler's thought process

It is important to remember that Hitler was an **ideologue**: he believed in the power of ideas, and race and space were his driving obsessions. He passionately believed in his long-term objectives and he passionately believed they were right. He also believed that he had the will to achieve them. Yet at the same time he also seems to have subscribed to a form of **determinism**. Thus, he believed that he had been chosen by 'Destiny' or 'Providence' (his words) to carry out these objectives and that success was assured (later when things went wrong he adopted a contrary **fatalism**). Now when he started to achieve success after success, this seemed to underline the determinism of his actions and he began to believe he could do no wrong; he began to speed up the process and, as we shall see, he became reckless.

Key terms

Ideologue
A theorist, one who believes in a particular system of ideas or rather a doctrinaire adherent of an ideology.

Determinism
The belief that everything is preordained.

Fatalism
Submission to what ever happens, believing it to be inevitable.

A change of behaviour?

This increasing urgency – almost impulsiveness – that we detect in 1938 was brought about not only by the narrowing range of options imposed on Hitler by economic restraints and other countries' rearmament (see page 141), but by his fear of an early death. In this case he feared 'Fate' would not allow him to fulfil his great tasks, which seems to contradict the previous idea that he had been chosen. Be that as it may, historians such as Joachim Fest and John Lukacs have identified a change of behaviour in 1938; for example, Hitler dictated a very detailed private will (2 May 1938), he shunned physical exercise, changed his eating and drinking habits, withdrew from much conviviality and concentrated more and more on foreign policy and preparation for war, although his experience at Munich convinced him, erroneously as it turned out, that the democratic leaders would not go to war over Poland.

Study Guide: Advanced-level Questions

In the style of AQA

In this paper you are given one and a half hours to read the three sources and answer the three questions. You are advised to devote 45 minutes to question (c).

Read the following sources and then answer the questions that follow.

Source A

Adapted from: J. Laver, Hitler – Germany's Fate or Germany's Misfortune?, *published in 1995*.

The next few years after 1933 were spent rearming, although the perception of Hitler and his generals appears to have been different: they wished to use the army possibly to bargain a revision of Versailles in Germany's favour; Hitler was probably more ambitious. The remilitarisation of the Rhineland seems to have been a decisive turning point. German sources themselves suggest that this was the last occasion when the Germans could have been stopped with relative ease. But Hitler had succeeded in his coup. From March 1936 onwards his strategy was more offensive.

Source B

From the Hossbach Memorandum, November 1937.

The aim of German policy was to make secure and to preserve the racial community and to enlarge it. ... German policy had to reckon with two hate-inspired antagonists, Britain and France, to whom a German colossus in the centre of Europe was a thorn in the flesh, and both countries were opposed to any further strengthening of Germany's position either in Europe or overseas. Germany's problem could only be solved by means of force, and this was never without risk. There still remains the questions 'when' and 'how'.

Source C

Adapted from: R. Henig, The Origins of the Second World War, published in 1985.

There is general agreement amongst historians that the ambitions of Hitler constitute the major element in the outbreak of war in 1939. His was the primary, if not the sole, responsibility. Considerable room for argument remains, however, about Hitler's aims and methods, about the degree to which he cold-bloodedly planned for war in pursuit of a German empire in the east, or seized opportunities that came to him, or was a compulsive gambler who took risks for even higher stakes.

(a) **Use Source A and your own knowledge**
How valid is the view in this source of the significance of the remilitarisation of the Rhineland? (10 marks)
(b) **Use Source B and your own knowledge**
How useful is this source as evidence of the aims of Nazi foreign policy? (10 marks)
(c) **Use Sources A, B and C and your own knowledge**
'Hitler's foreign policy up to 1939 was carefully planned and consistently carried out, making war in Europe inevitable.' Assess the validity of this opinion. (20 marks)

Source: AQA, June 2004

Exam tips

The cross-references are intended to take you straight to the material that will help you to answer the questions.

This exemplar AQA question is designed to test your understanding of the views of different historians about Hitler's foreign policy and the origins of the Second World War. The source extracts have been chosen to offer a variety of views and the series of questions is designed to test recall (i.e. memory/knowledge) and comprehension (your understanding of the views expressed in the source). You should make an overall assessment, combining an evaluation of all the sources with your knowledge in response to a specific question. In this instance question **(a)** is concerned with the validity of the interpretation in the source; **(b)** with the usefulness of the source; while **(c)** requires you to use all three sources to evaluate an opinion. In each answer emphasis is placed on the use of your own knowledge in addition to the source(s), and the historiographical context of this paper means that you would also be expected to refer to the opinions of other historians in your answers, particularly to part **(c)**.

(a) In this question you are required to understand and evaluate the interpretation and relate it to your own knowledge to reach a sustained and well-supported judgement on its validity. You should start by identifying the interpretation and should then consider its validity.

- Could Hitler have been stopped in the Rhineland (page 36)?
- Was this move any more decisive than conscription or rearmament?
- Hitler did nothing for 2 years after this. Were not Austria and Czechoslovakia more decisive (pages 74 and 76)?
- Could he have still been stopped in 1938?

(b) In this question you are required to evaluate the strengths and limitations of the source to reach a judgement in relation to its utility (note this question is about utility, on other papers it could be reliability; candidates are not expected to do both!) so as to answer the issue in the question. You should consider 'utility' with reference to provenance and context as well as considering the content of the source.

- On the one hand you could decide this was a clear expression of Hitler's long-term intentions *vis-à-vis* race and space.
- Or, you could argue it was not a formal declaration of policy, not a proper record and no decisions were taken.
- You could cite the historical debate (page 73) and you could point forward to what happened in 1938.

Whatever your line of argument you should try to reach a conclusion about the source's utility – ensuring that you are precise about 'what it doesn't say' and what the historian can learn from it.

(c) In the final question you obviously need to refer to all the sources and your own knowledge in a precise way to respond to the question as well as showing your historiographical understanding.

- The personality of Hitler dominates the debate: was his fanatical will the driving force behind a consistent programme of aggression or was he weaker, less decisive, responding to events (page 83)?
- Clearly, the historical debate as well as the sources are relevant here (page 85).

In the style of Edexcel

In the paper you are given an hour to write a single essay for which 60 marks are awarded. There will be a choice of two questions. Here is one relevant to the chapter you have just read.

To what extent did German Foreign Policy become more openly 'Nazi', rather than purely nationalist, in the course of 1938?

Source: Edexcel, June 2002

Exam tips

The cross-references are intended to take you straight to the material that will help you to answer the question.

See pages 16, 19 and 22–3 for some general advice on essay-writing skills.

This is not an easy question. The real issue here is the distinction between nationalist foreign policy and Nazi foreign policy, i.e. the difference between the general desire to overthrow Versailles and restore German pride, and ideas more specific to Hitler, which revolved around race and space. And the emphasis on the year 1938. Clearly you will need to:

- Define nationalist foreign policy common to the Weimar and Nazi regimes (re-read Chapter 2).
- Evaluate Hitler's actions in terms of their relationship to the Versailles Treaty, i.e. rearmament, conscription, the occupation of the Rhineland (re-read Chapter 2); but be careful, the main focus should be on 1938.
- Define what is more specifically Nazi in terms of foreign policy aims (re-read Chapter 2).
- Evaluate the *Anschluss* and the partial occupation of Czechoslovakia and decide, given that neither had been part of the Second Reich, whether or not these actions represent a departure from traditional nationalist policy (re-read this chapter).
- Reach a reasoned judgement.

5 Appeasement

POINTS TO CONSIDER

This chapter gives a broad overview of French and British foreign policy as well as a look at the historiography of appeasement. You should try to appreciate the difficulties facing the democracies' policy-makers in the 1930s and then you will be better able to judge the historians' verdict.

The key areas examined are:

- Appeasement: an introduction
- French foreign policy explained
- British foreign policy explained
- Appeasement: the debate

Key dates

1919	August	Britain adopted the Ten-Year Rule
1929		Maginot Line begun
	October 3	Death of Gustav Stresemann
	October 29	Wall Street Crash
1931	September 18	Japan invaded Manchuria
1932	March	Ten-Year Rule ended
1933		Defence Requirements Committee set up in UK
1934		British rearmament began
1935	April 11–14	Stresa Front
	May 2	Franco-Soviet Pact
	June 18	Anglo-German Naval Agreement
	October 3	Mussolini invaded Abyssinia
1936		France's Popular Front government began rearmament
	March 7	Remilitarisation of the Rhineland
	July 18	Spanish Civil War broke out
1937		Chamberlain accelerated rearmament
1938	March 12	*Anschluss*: Hitler occupies Austria
	September 29	Munich Conference
1939	February	Britain committed to France

1 | Appeasement: An Introduction

Key question
What was
appeasement?

Appeasement is most commonly associated with the policy of
Neville Chamberlain, British Prime Minister from 1937 to 1940.
More specifically, it is associated with the Munich crisis of 1938
and the failure to prevent the outbreak of war in 1939. Indeed,
far from preventing war, appeasement appeared to bring it about
by encouraging Hitler to make greater demands. Quite clearly the
policy failed and it failed spectacularly. Mainly because of this, it
came to be seen as a dishonourable policy, a policy of peace at
any price, a policy of **craven acquiescence** in the demands of a
bullying dictator. It became, in fact, a byword for cowardice, a
pejorative term.

But this is not what the word meant in origin: most dictionaries
usually define appeasement as pacification or conciliation, and
that is what Foreign Secretary Anthony Eden meant in 1936 when
he stated to the House of Commons, 'it is the appeasement of
Europe as a whole that we have constantly before us', meaning,
quite simply, that he wished to make Europe a peaceful place.
British policy was in fact mainly just that – keeping the peace –
and it was prepared to do that by satisfying reasonable grievances,
by making concessions to avoid war.

**Craven
acquiescence**
Giving in, in a
cowardly fashion.

Pejorative
A word depreciated
in value, a word
used disparagingly.

Key terms

A popular policy

Before 1938 appeasement was a policy approved by practically
everyone. It had been the principal characteristic of British
foreign policy from the Treaty of Versailles onwards, for it did not
take long for anti-German feeling in Britain to subside after the
war and, when it did, a feeling grew that the harshness of the
treaty could be progressively modified by negotiation and
concession. Opposition to the French occupation of the Ruhr
(1923), support for the Dawes and Young Plans (1924 and 1929)
and the Locarno Treaty (1925), the removal of weapons
inspectors from Germany (1927), the withdrawal of troops from
the Rhineland (1930) and the virtual cancellation of reparations
in 1932 were all part of a piece: remove Germany's grievances
and there will be no war. In addition, by the 1930s most
historians were contending that Germany was not solely
responsible for the First World War, thus removing any remaining
moral justification for the Treaty of Versailles.

Appeasement, then, was not a policy of peace at any price: it
was in fact a rational policy based on a wide variety of
considerations, considerations that will be discussed later in the
chapter. Appeasement was, above all, a British policy, but in the
later 1930s it was a policy that the French also came to adopt.
Quite why is the subject of the next section.

Key question
To what extent did the French policy change in the 1920s?

2 | French Foreign Policy Explained

Although victorious, France had been devastated by the war and the determination to exact revenge soon gave way to a feeling of pessimism about the future.

The 1920s

How had France been affected by the war? Here are the major consequences:

- colossal debts had been incurred ($4 billion to the USA and $3 billion to Britain)
- about 10 per cent of France had been laid waste, affecting some of the most valuable industrial and agricultural resources
- more importantly, a million and half men had been killed (10 per cent of active males; the highest proportion of all the major belligerents) and another three million wounded
- the large-scale loss of life not only had an adverse **demographic** effect on a static and ageing population, but it also left deep psychological scars: parents, grandparents, wives, girlfriends, brothers, sisters and children all experienced the grief of lost loved ones – there can have been few who were untouched by the experience.

Key terms

Demographic
Relating to population level.

Punitive
Extremely severe.

The Tiger?

Accordingly there was immense pressure on the Prime Minister, Georges Clemenceau, whose nickname was 'the Tiger', to deliver a **punitive** peace which would render Germany harmless in the future. But so far from being the tough negotiator of textbook fame, Clemenceau abandoned all thought of dismembering Germany or of a permanent French occupation of the Rhineland on the flimsy assurance of an Anglo-American guarantee of future French security (which never came to pass). Thus, he succumbed to a lenient peace and was roundly criticised, especially by Marshal Ferdinand Foch, for giving away too much. The French could be forgiven for seeing Clemenceau as more of a pussy-cat than a tiger.

The peace was accepted by both parliament and people with grim resignation and by the end of 1919 many saw the peace merely as an armistice, a truce for 20 years as the famous cartoon overleaf so poignantly implied. For in truth the German problem had not been resolved: Germany's larger population (60 million as opposed to 40 million, but a ratio of two to one in the 20–34-year age group by 1940) and greater industrial capacity meant that in any rerun of the contest the Germans would probably come out on top.

Little *Entente*

France, therefore, needed allies and, in the absence of a strong League of Nations and a deal with Britain, signed a series of bilateral agreements through the 1920s with Belgium (1920), Poland (1921 and 1925), Czechoslovakia (1924), Romania (1926)

PEACE AND FUTURE CANNON FODDER

The Tiger : "Curious ! I seem to hear a child weeping ! "

A cartoon from the *Daily Herald*, 1919. The Tiger is saying: 'Curious! I seem to hear a child weeping.' Behind Clemenceau are (left to right): the prime ministers Lloyd George of Britain, Orlando of Italy and President Woodrow Wilson of the USA. The artist is most prescient in suggesting that those who will be of military age in 1940 will suffer the consequences of an unsatisfactory peace: another conflagration.

and Yugoslavia (1927). The last three were known as the 'Little *Entente*', although how valuable these were is a moot point.

Ruhr occupation

In addition it was decided to take a tough line against Germany and rigidly enforce the terms of Versailles. The famous occupation of the Ruhr in 1923 was just the last, most spectacular example of this policy. It is often forgotten that French troops were sent across the Rhine to enforce German compliance several times during the course of 1920–1.

A series of agreements

The Ruhr occupation turned out to be a defeat for France as well as a disaster for Germany (see page 15). It paved the way for a period of appeasement signalled by the Dawes Plan of 1924 and the Locarno Agreements of 1925 and later the Young Plan of 1929 and the evacuation of French troops from the Rhineland in

Key dates

Work began on the
Maginot Line: 1929

Death of Gustav
Stresemann:
3 October 1929

Wall Street Crash:
29 October 1929

Key term

Maginot Line
A line of defensive
fortifications along
France's north-
eastern border from
Switzerland to
Luxemburg named
after the French
War Minister, André
Maginot. It was
completed in the
late 1930s, but
easily outflanked in
1940.

Key question
To what extent and
why did French policy
come to rely on
Britain in the 1930s?

Key dates

Japan invaded
Manchuria:
18 September 1931

Stresa Front:
11–14 April 1935

Franco-Soviet Pact:
2 May 1935

1930. The policy of conciliation and compromise is most associated with Aristide Briand, who was Foreign Minister between 1925 and 1931. However, as time passed, obstacles to his policy came to the fore. The death of Stresemann and the Wall Street Crash (both in 1929) created instability and unease. Yet whereas in the aftermath of the Versailles Treaty French strategy had been based on offensive action to counter the German threat, by 1929 policy had changed completely. It was now entirely defensive.

Maginot Line
This was signalled by the start of the **Maginot Line** in that year, although the much-derided fortifications were not designed to protect the whole of France, just Alsace-Lorraine. The German attack was always expected to come through Belgium, where the bulk of the French army was to be. However, the problem lay not so much with the Maginot Line itself, but with the passive and defensive mentality it came to represent. The French wrongly believed in the superiority of defence over attack, which had, of course, been true for the previous war, but which took insufficient account of technological developments since, especially the offensive potential of tanks and aircraft.

The 1930s
The new decade was ushered in with disappointment at the failure of the League of Nations to cope with Japan's invasion of Manchuria in 1931 (see page 18). From the French point of view it made little sense to agree to arms reductions at the long-awaited Disarmament Conference in this climate, especially when the German government continued to flout the Versailles agreement, and especially when Germany came under 'new and dangerous management' (Bell) from 1933.

The impact of the Depression
Compared with Britain or Germany, France had been less affected by the Depression in the years 1929–32 (being less dependent on trade), but it struck later, peaking in 1935, and there was no recovery until 1938. Historians have identified a dramatic collapse in French standing between 1933 and 1937 coinciding with this economic crisis. There was (always) considerable ministerial instability (11 governments between 1932 and 1935; all of them weak coalitions) and France was politically divided (some would say it had been since 1789!). This was because of the rival ideologies of Communism and Fascism, which in 1935 made France look first one way (to Fascist Italy in the Stresa Front and later for a military agreement) then the other (to the Soviet Union also for an alliance). There was rarely any continuity or consistency in foreign affairs and, as a result, particular policies were often not carried through to their logical conclusion: paralysis could be the result. This, together with a general feeling of revulsion against war, weakened French reactions to Hitler and in fact encouraged him by presenting no opposition.

Rhineland and after

The remilitarisation of the Rhineland in 1936 (see page 36) came as no surprise in France and caused little consternation. However, it did cause the Belgians to revoke their military **accord** and opt for **neutrality**, thus presenting the French high command with a dilemma over their strategy (they took the easy way out and decided to change nothing). Other setbacks followed. As a consequence of the Abyssinian crisis (see page 52), Italy drifted towards Germany, a process accelerated by the Spanish Civil War; negotiations with the Soviet Union seemed to be going nowhere; and Britain remained as non-committal as ever. The threat to French security was by now very real: the German army was thought to be certainly the equal of the French and the air force superior.

Rearmament

Accordingly, in the autumn of 1936 the left-wing **Popular Front** government launched the first serious substantial rearmament effort in the interwar period: 31 billion francs were spent over the next 3 years. More tension came in 1938 as Austria was annexed and Czechoslovakia dismembered. By this time, French policy was in the hands of Foreign Minster Georges Bonnet and Prime Minister Édouard Daladier. However, whereas Bonnet was an arch-appeaser, Daladier was not: he was disgusted by the Munich settlement and for him it was something of a turning point.

Yet French policy remained one of appeasement until Britain finally made a firm continental commitment to France in February 1939 (see page 106). At this point Daladier stepped up rearmament and was quick to agree to military discussions with the British chiefs of staff. Now French opinion hardened against Hitler, and after February 1939 French policy was characterised by a resolution and confidence that had not been present for many years.

Analysis of French foreign policy

Most analysis of French foreign policy in the interwar period has been coloured by France's rapid collapse in 1940. This was such a disaster that (so the argument goes) it had to be the outcome of deep-seated political, social and economic weaknesses. Accordingly, historians have searched for all manner of divisions and examples of decadence, corruption, pacifism and incompetence, and they have not been disappointed. From this point of view, France deserved defeat in 1940, it had it coming. However, if perhaps the defeat was largely just the result of superior German military strategy in the month of May 1940, then this whole approach is quite false and the debate it has generated is meaningless. Now this is not to say that France did not have weaknesses, they were there in abundance, but it is just to say that their importance has been exaggerated by the all-too-familiar mistake of reading history backwards.

Key terms

Accord
Agreement.

Neutrality
Not supporting either side in a conflict.

Popular Front
An alliance of French Communist, radical and socialist elements.

Key dates

Mussolini invaded Abyssinia: 3 October 1935

Remilitarisation of the Rhineland: 7 March 1936

Outbreak of the Spanish Civil War: 18 July 1936

France's Popular Front government began rearmament: 1936

Anschluss – Hitler occupied Austria: 12 March 1938

Munich Conference: 29 September 1938

Britain committed to France: February 1939

Key question
Was France's collapse in 1940 the result of a long-term malaise, or was it just a sudden military defeat?

Key terms

Third Republic
The republican regime in France between the fall of Napoleon III in 1870 and the German occupation of 1940.

Proportional representation
An electoral system in which parties gain seats in proportion to the number of votes cast for them. It is therefore very difficult for a single party to gain a majority (i.e. 51 per cent of the vote).

Political instability

Nevertheless, there is no doubt that the politics of government in the **Third Republic** were quite chaotic. Forty-three prime ministers between 1917 and 1940 does not create much political continuity in terms of policy and decision-making. Why was this? The answer seems to be the voting system of **proportional representation**, which generated a large number of parties, none of which could obtain a majority. For instance, in 1938 there were 17 political groups in the Chamber from which some sort of government had to be formed. This sort of situation meant that governments had to be cobbled together by compromise and concession; clearly most were fragile coalitions with a short life. There was also, as we have already seen, a considerable political divide between the right and the left that severely damaged foreign policy. On the left there was a strong strain of pacifism, and a revulsion against war among the population at large (particularly the peasantry). This in turn served to hamper any attempt at rearmament.

It took a change of heart by the left in 1936 to get rearmament under way. It was the Popular Front government that recognised the threat Hitler posed and dropped the policy of pacifism. Of course, it turned out to be a case of too little, too late, but it is rather difficult in a democracy to put the economy on a war footing when you do not know when there is going to be a war. Living standards suffer and appeasement is a lot cheaper.

Germany: the enemy

There was no real debate about who the enemy was. Everyone knew it was Germany. But there was precious little consensus about how to deal with the problem. How could France cope with a resurgent Germany? Should it take a tough line or should it appease? French ambivalence was caused by a lack of options. France was not strong enough to act alone; it needed allies, but who would make the best ally? The 'Little *Entente*' (Czechoslovakia, Romania and Yugoslavia) was of little value; it could never have amounted to a deterrent to German expansion in Eastern Europe. An agreement with Fascist Italy was opposed by the left (and was, in any case, also of dubious value) and an agreement with the Soviet Union was opposed by the right and Britain, although both were attempted.

Britain: the unreliable friend

In fact, the key to French defence policy was Britain, a factor not fully appreciated by historians until the French archives were opened up in the early 1970s. France could not risk a war without Britain's support. France needed Britain for its navy, air force (the French air force had been badly neglected) and immense resources. The French believed the next war was going to be like the last one. France would have to defend its borders against the German onslaught; this would be halted and then the war would become one of attrition that Germany could not win, but Britain and France, with their superior resources, could. The problem with this diagnosis was that Britain was not party to the plan and was wholly self-interested and unreliable (an example of this behaviour can be seen in the Anglo-German Naval Agreement in June 1935, page 34).

This explains why French policy was often so indecisive. The French had to wait for British initiatives and they had to fall in behind British policy if the situation became perilous. For instance, Italian friendship was sacrificed to accommodate Britain's foreign policy over Abyssinia. France's problem was that it could not predict what Britain would do, just as France could not predict what Hitler was going to do. This is why policy was often ineffectual and ambivalent. French policy came to depend on what Hitler and Chamberlain decided. It was essentially a reactive policy, and it is hard to see any alternatives. Thus, France adopted a policy of appeasement because Britain did.

Anglo-German Naval Agreement: 18 June 1935

Key date

A turning point

The aftermath of Munich turned out to be a major turning point for both Britain and France. Now, at last, Britain recognised the menace of Hitler and from February 1939 was prepared to work with the French to resist it. As 1939 progressed, morale in France was quite good. The German menace could no longer be ignored and the people were united in resistance to it. Pacifism was now the policy of only a small minority. The revulsion against war remained, but now the feeling was that conflict might not be avoided. The people were fed up with German threats and German lies. Hitler had created a level of consensus among the French people not seen since the previous war. And with Britain at its side there was a quiet confidence that all would be well.

Conclusion

If French policy is characterised by ambivalence and indecision in these years, that is understandable. France had been out of its depth since 1919, cast in an international role for which it lacked adequate resources, faced with a resurgent Germany and with little idea how to proceed. Firmness risked war; concession seemed to do the same. From the mid-1930s onwards there was a general feeling that the nation's interests were everywhere imperilled and that only the support of Britain would enable France to meet the main threat with confidence. The British slowly came to the view that the Anglo-French alliance would have to be reactivated if Germany got out of hand, but without being willing to say as much to the French. Similarly the French developed a strategy for wartime that was entirely based on British support, but without actually being assured of that support. It was fortunate for both nations that eventually their interests came to coincide.

Summary diagram: French foreign policy explained

1920s

France weakened by First World War

Versailles, a disappointment

Small-scale agreements

Ruhr occupation

Locarno honeymoon

1929 Crash

Maginot mentality

1930s

Political instability

Economic depression

1936 Rearmament

Appeasement

Closer ties with Britain

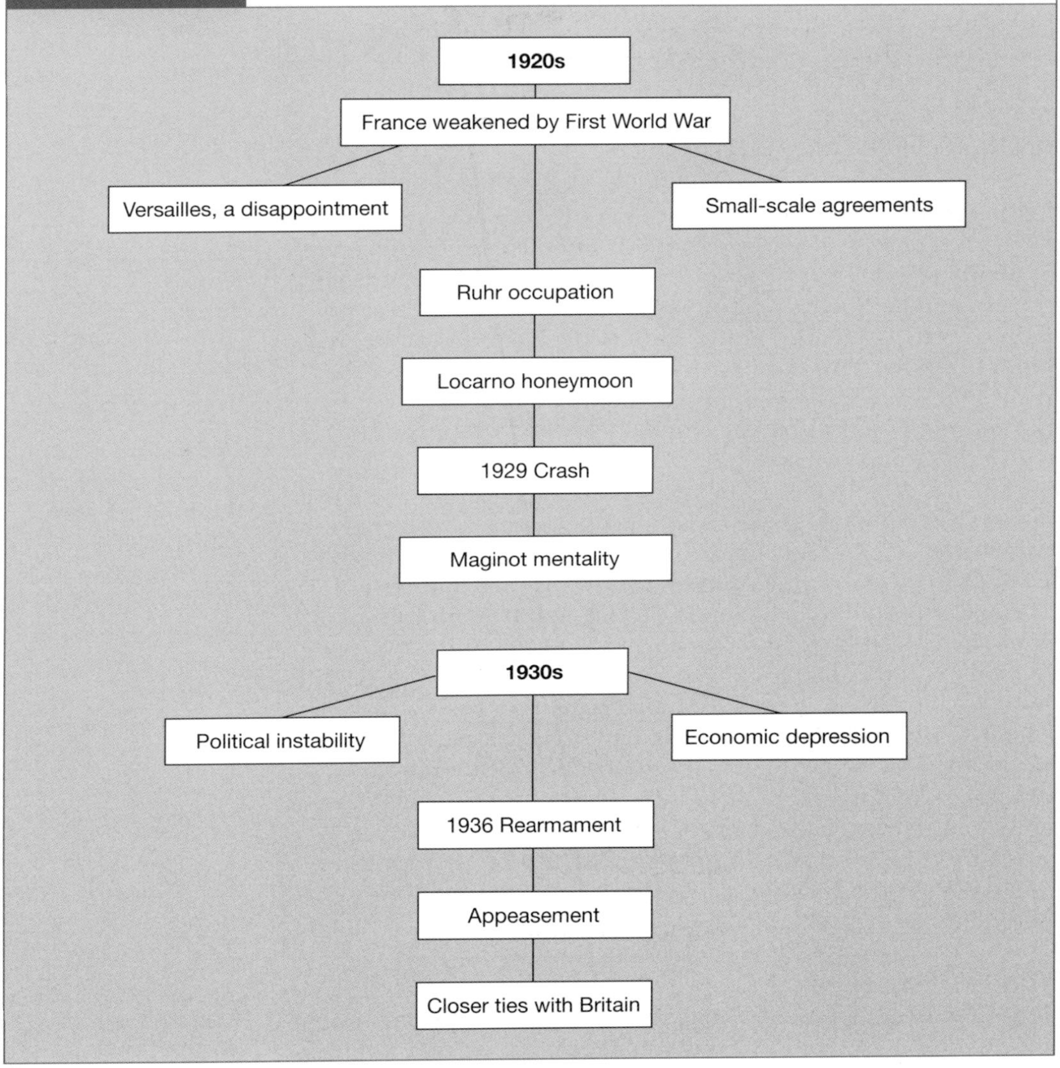

Key question
What characterised British policy in the 1920s?

3 | British Foreign Policy Explained

The 1920s

Weakness

Like France, Britain was devastated by the experience of the First World War. Although its losses were half that of its neighbour, the deaths of 750,000 young men had had an equally traumatic effect. In the aftermath there was a widespread feeling that carnage on such a scale should not be allowed to happen again, that never again should Britain send an army to the continent, and that the last war would be just that, 'the war to end all wars', as H.G. Wells (nearly) put it. The feeling also grew that the conflict had been largely futile.

In addition, Britain had been devastated economically: debts had mushroomed to over £7 billion, export markets had been lost, and traditional industries such as textiles and shipbuilding went into decline. Clearly Britain could neither face nor afford another war.

Prestige

And yet British prestige was very high, higher than it had been for a very long time. With the addition of some of Germany's African colonies and some of Turkey's middle eastern provinces as **mandates**, the British Empire now reached its greatest extent, covering about 25 per cent of the globe. The map was truly painted red, as a glance at the (admittedly black and white) map opposite shows. However, this growth only served to mask the reality, for there was an enormous disparity between commitments and resources.

Britain's global responsibilities were in fact a logistical nightmare. A general staff minute of 1921 stated; 'our liabilities are so vast ... that to assess them must be largely a matter of conjecture'. For instance, apart from the defence of the British Isles, the (self-governing) **dominions** of Australia and New Zealand expected to be defended by the Royal Navy, Palestine alone tied down 20,000 troops during a rebellion in 1938, and the bulk of forces had to be stationed in India where the growing tide of nationalism seemed to threaten the very basis of British rule. Britain could not possibly defend such a disparate, widespread set of territories. Moreover, the Empire was not a coherent structure; there was no common economic policy, no agreed system of decision-making, no co-ordinated defence structure. The larger the Empire became, the more impressive it looked on paper, but the more difficult it became to administer and defend.

The Ten-Year Rule

It was fortunate for Britain that in the immediate aftermath of the war the vulnerability of the Empire was not a major problem. With some justification the cabinet agreed in August 1919 that:

> It should be assumed ... that the British Empire will not be engaged in any great war during the next 10 years, and that no **Expeditionary Force** is required for this purpose.

Dramatic cuts were made in armed forces expenditure, e.g. from £692 million in 1919–20 to £115 million by 1922, and this Ten-Year Rule, as it was known, came to be extended beyond 1929. Rearmament did not get under way again until 1934.

Revisionism

From the moment the Peace of Paris was signed, the British government was **revisionist**. As early as March 1919 Lloyd George warned against treating Germany too harshly and the influential economist J.M. Keynes emphasised that European

---

Key terms

Mandates
Territories administered on behalf of the League of Nations.

Dominions
In the context of the Empire, the (white) self-governing territories with the same head of state.

Key date

Britain adopted the Ten-Year Rule: August 1919

Key terms

Expeditionary Force
A mobile army to be sent to the European continent.

Revisionist
Wishing to re-examine, alter and correct something.

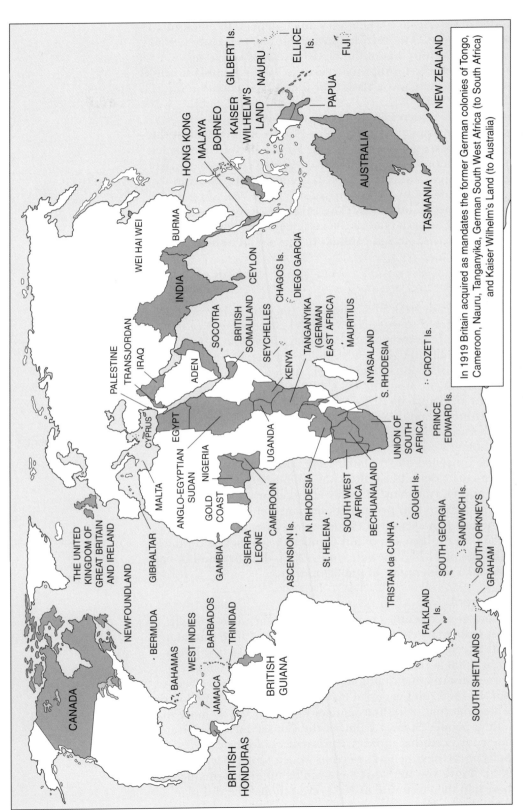

In 1919 Britain acquired as mandates the former German colonies of Tongo, Cameroon, Nauru, Tanganyika, German South West Africa (to South Africa) and Kaiser Wilhelm's Land (to Australia)

The British Empire 1920. (Shaded and named countries are countries within the Empire.)

economic prosperity as a whole very much depended on German economic recovery. The British approach to the peace, then, was rather different from that of the French as it was based on economic self-interest rather than security. In this context it is not surprising that there was a clash over the Ruhr occupation in 1923 (see page 15).

Indeed, Britain increasingly saw itself as neutral between France and Germany rather than allied to the former against the latter. After Locarno it was hoped that Europe could safely be left to solve its own problems, but by the early 1930s it was clear that detachment might not keep the peace. As the world situation deteriorated, rocked by the repercussions of the Wall Street Crash, Britain could not stand idly by. The British government still believed it had a special moral role as a leader in world affairs, a legacy of that Victorian self-confidence that would be slow to fade.

The 1930s

Japan

As we have already indicated, when the Ten-Year Rule was up in 1929, it was agreed to extend it. In any event, the onset of the Depression made rearmament a financial impossibility. The crucial event that changed British policy was Japan's invasion of Manchuria in 1931. Japan had been an ally of Britain's since 1902, but, under pressure from the USA, Lloyd George had given up the Japanese alliance in 1921 at the Washington Conference. This had deprived Britain of any means of influencing Japanese policy without substituting any compensating support from the USA.

The cabinet reluctantly concluded that the Ten-Year Rule should be cancelled on 23 March 1932 and in 1933 a Defence Requirements Committee (DRC) was established to advise on strategy and rearmament. Manchuria was clearly a defeat for the League of Nations and privately politicians were aware of its ineffectuality. However, the League was very popular with the public and in this new era of full democracy (all men and women over the age of 21 had the vote from 1928), the government had to take much more notice of public opinion.

Rearmament

Rearmament on the other hand did not appear to be popular; in the East Fulham by-election of 1933 the Conservative candidate who advocated rearmament turned a majority of 14,000 into a defeat by 5000 at the hands of his Labour opponent who supported disarmament (although other issues were involved, of course). In 1935 the League of Nations Union's 'Peace Ballot' that advocated international disarmament was endorsed by more than 11 million people. Stanley Baldwin, the Conservative leader, became convinced that rapid rearmament would mean defeat at the polls in the next general election (which took place at the end of 1935). 'I give you my word there will be no great armaments', Baldwin told the electorate in 1935, even though he did plan some rearmament.

Key question
Why did the Ten-Year Rule finally come to an end?

Key dates

Ten-Year Rule ended: March 1932

Defence Requirements Committee set up in UK: 1933

British rearmament began: 1934

Germany and the RAF

The DRC produced its first report in February 1934 and identified Germany as 'the ultimate potential enemy', pushing Japan and naval considerations into second place. It recommended the establishment of an Expeditionary Force, but the cabinet felt that public opinion would be hostile to this. Instead, priority was given to building up the Royal Air Force (RAF), which the cabinet's dominant figure, the Chancellor Neville Chamberlain, saw as the best deterrent against Germany. The DRC reported again in November 1935, by which time Hitler's rearmament programme was public knowledge and the Abyssinian crisis was turning Mussolini, a potential ally, into a potential enemy. It stated:

> It is a cardinal requirement of our National and Imperial security that our foreign policy should be so conducted as to avoid the possible development of a situation in which we might be confronted simultaneously with the hostility of Japan in the Far East, Germany in the West, and any power on the main line of communication between the two.

In March 1936 its conclusions formed the basis of a 4-year plan for rearmament that Chamberlain accelerated when he came into office. Expenditure leapt from £185 million in 1936 to £719 million in 1939.

Stanley Baldwin, Prime Minister 1935–7

Aware of current British weakness and acting on the advice of the DRC and defence chiefs, Stanley Baldwin, Prime Minister from June 1935, did his best to avoid any crisis. In this context he and his predecessor MacDonald acquiesced in Hitler's reintroduction of conscription and remilitarisation of the Rhineland, attached little importance to the Stresa declaration, signed a naval agreement with Germany, which upset the French, did little to prevent Mussolini taking Abyssinia (but enough to lose his friendship) and stayed out of the Spanish Civil War, thus giving the dictators a free hand.

With hindsight, these policy decisions (if they can be so called) look like failures, but they have to be seen in the context of Britain's military weakness and global concerns. Where perhaps Baldwin did err was in being too ready to accommodate public opinion; he tended to follow rather than mould it, but perhaps that is one of the functions of a democratic politician. Another problem was the fact that the government seemed to be caught off guard by each successive crisis and was constantly reacting to events rather than having any influence over how they might develop. When he became Prime Minister in May 1937, Neville Chamberlain was determined to inject more vigour and purpose in foreign affairs: he was prepared to take the initiative. Policy changed from passive to active appeasement.

Key date | Chamberlain accelerated rearmament: 1937

Neville Chamberlain, Prime Minister 1937–40

Chamberlain assumed much more responsibility for foreign affairs than had his predecessor, hoping to produce what he called a 'Grand Settlement' of international problems, to create 'a lasting European peace' through a concert orchestrated by Britain and involving France, Germany and Italy. This was based on the (false) assumption that Hitler was a reasonable man and that he could get a deal with Germany involving the possible return of colonies, an air pact and some resolution of Germany's grievances in Eastern Europe.

Chamberlain did not want to make any firm guarantees to France, he did not trust the Soviet Union, but he did put some

---

Profile: (Arthur) Neville Chamberlain 1869–1940

1869	–	Born in Birmingham, the son of the famous radical politician Joseph Chamberlain
1915–16	–	Lord Mayor of Birmingham
1917	–	Became Director General of National Service
1918	–	Elected as a Member of Parliament
1923–4	–	Appointed Chancellor of the Exchequer
1924–9	–	Appointed Minister for Health
1931–7	–	Appointed Chancellor of the Exchequer
1937–40	–	Served as Prime Minister
1940	–	Resigned in May; died in November

Neville Chamberlain was noted for his clear thinking, mastery of detail and hard work, but also for his impatience with criticism, his certainty in his own beliefs and his disdain for those who disagreed with him. As prime minister he devoted much of his energy to foreign policy, although he had little experience of it. He is, of course, primarily associated with the policy of appeasement that found its basis in his personal fear of war, his appreciation of Britain's limitations and his belief that Germany's grievances were genuine. As he said at the time of Munich: 'Armed conflict is a nightmare to me … I shall not give up hope of a peaceful solution, or abandon my efforts for peace, as long as any chance for peace remains' (from his radio broadcast of 27 September 1938).

But Chamberlain misread Hitler and his policy failed. With the invasion of Poland a year later, Chamberlain was forced to declare war. He acknowledged the failure of his policy: 'This is a sad day for all of us, and to none is it sadder than to me. Everything that I have worked for, everything that I have hoped for, everything that I believed in during my public life, has crashed into ruins. … I trust I may live to see the day when Hitlerism has been destroyed, and a liberated Europe has been re-established' (from his address to Parliament on 3 September 1939).

Sadly Chamberlain did not live to see the end of Hitler. He stood down as prime minister in May 1940 to make way for Winston Churchill, and he died of cancer, a broken man, on 9 November 1940.

(misplaced) trust in Mussolini, whom he felt might restrain Hitler. Early in 1938 the Foreign Secretary, Eden, resigned not because he opposed appeasement (although he opposed negotiations with Mussolini), but because of Chamberlain's determination to conduct foreign policy himself.

The military and financial context

Chamberlain's determination to achieve a peaceful settlement was to some extent influenced by wild overestimates of German rearmament and strength from the chiefs of staff. A particularly gloomy (and prescient) review of the international situation was produced by them in June 1937 in which the Italian threat in the Mediterranean was added to that of Germany in Europe and Japan in the Far East: 'the outstanding feature of the present situation is the increasing probability that a war started in one of these three areas may extend to one or both of the other two'. Their conclusion was that until rearmament was further advanced, it should be the first task of foreign policy to diminish the number of Britain's enemies.

The policy of 'appeasement' can only be fully understood if the military context is also fully understood. Since the summer of 1937, the Treasury too had been demanding a more positive attitude to Germany by the Foreign Office. In December 1937 Sir Thomas Inskip, a government minister with responsibility for co-ordinating defence, presented his 'Interim Report on Defence Expenditure in Future Years', inspired by Treasury fears that expenditure was becoming excessive. It is evident from the report that the stability of the British economy was considered of vital importance if Britain were to fight because it was believed the next encounter would again be a long **war of attrition**. Based on this premise, the priorities for defence were to be (in order of importance):

1. Military preparation sufficient to repulse air attacks.
2. The preservation of trade routes for the supply of food and raw materials.
3. The defence of the Empire.
4. The defence of any power or powers with whom Britain might be allied.

Little choice

As in 1934 priority was given to the RAF, but the cabinet now changed the strategy. Priority was given to the construction of a fighter force; the bombers were now of less importance. This was justified on the grounds that the development of **radar** made the interception of enemy bombers feasible. In January 1938 the chiefs of staff presented a review that reiterated what had been stated in the summer memorandum:

> Naval, Military and Air Forces in their present stage of development, are still far from sufficient to meet our defensive commitments, which now extend from western Europe, through the Mediterranean

Key terms

War of attrition
A war in which one side wins by gradually wearing down the other with repeated attacks, etc.

Radar
A system for detecting objects by means of radio waves. In this context, a method of air defence.

A cartoon by Jimmy Friell ('Gabriel') published in the *Daily Worker* newspaper, September 1938.

to the Far East. … We cannot foresee the time when our defence forces will be strong enough to safeguard our territory, trade and vital interests against Germany, Italy and Japan simultaneously.

These observations together with the financial constraints placed on rearmament no doubt convinced the Prime Minister that the conciliation of Germany and Italy was the only viable policy: they presented him with little choice.

The Czech crisis

Chamberlain had come into office determined to take the initiative, but the *Anschluss* with Austria took him by surprise (as it did Hitler!). He did not object to the union, but he disliked the way it had happened. Still, he felt it made appeasement all the more urgent. In a statement to the House of Commons on 24 March 1938, Chamberlain stated that the next crisis would be over Czechoslovakia and while he could not guarantee that state (nor automatically come to the aid of France, its ally), he did point out that if a war did break out, Britain might not be able to stay out of it.

Of course, this veiled threat was meant to be a **deterrent**; Chamberlain's real aim was to achieve a peaceful settlement, and his three flights to Germany in the autumn indicate the lengths to which he was prepared to go. However, the real problem was that Chamberlain took Hitler's demand for the Sudetenland at face value; he believed Hitler just wanted to unite all Germans. After meeting him for the first time, he wrote to his sister: 'I got the impression that here was a man who could be relied on when he had given his word.' But just a week later Hitler had raised the stakes. War now seemed likely and Chamberlain even undertook to support France in war if the French decided to fight for the Czechs. However, his real reluctance can be gauged from his

Deterrent
Something that puts someone off from doing something.

Key term

radio broadcast to the nation on the evening of 28 September 1938:

> How horrible, fantastic, incredible it is that we should be digging trenches and trying on gas masks here because of a quarrel in a far-away country between people of whom we know nothing ... war is a fearful thing, and we must be very clear, before we embark on it, that it is really the great issues that are at stake.

The peacemaker?

It is clear from his radio broadcast that Chamberlain did not want a war over this issue (see the critical cartoon opposite) and when the opportunity came for a conference at Munich he leapt at it. When he returned with 'peace for our time', he was greeted as a hero by both press and people, and was bombarded with letters of congratulation (over 40,000) and gifts (including very many umbrellas; see the flattering cartoon from *Punch* below). However, in the House of Commons the debate over the settlement elicited strong criticism from Churchill, Attlee and others. Although the government won the vote, the debate was seen as a defeat. The

'Still hope'. A cartoon from *Punch*, September 1938.

policy looked as threadbare as it actually was. Indeed the criticism articulated in the Commons presaged a dramatic change of mood in Britain, which had already been anticipated by divisions in cabinet.

For Britain, and to a lesser extent France, Munich turned out to be the limit of the policy of concession. Peace at any price was never the policy of Chamberlain or his cabinet; the British government would not accept German domination of Europe. Chamberlain still placed some faith in negotiation and believed he might be able to influence Hitler through Mussolini, but his visit to Rome in January 1939 achieved little.

A change of policy

Indeed it was the Foreign Secretary, Halifax, who took the lead in urging a tougher policy towards Germany; on 25 January 1939 he warned that Hitler might attack in the west. On 1 February the cabinet agreed that Britain must go to war if Germany invaded either the Netherlands or Switzerland and agreed to staff talks with the French. On 6 February Chamberlain declared that 'any threat to the vital interests of France from whatever quarter it came must evoke the immediate co-operation of Great Britain'. Even more importantly, a paper by the chiefs of staff on 20 February argued that home defence might have to include a share in the defence of French territory. On 22 February the cabinet agreed to prepare an army of eight divisions for dispatch to the continent.

Thus, British policy was in the process of undergoing a dramatic change in February 1939. The previous assumption had been that Hitler's aims were limited. It was now feared that Hitler's ultimate aim was the domination of Europe, and he might have to be stopped. Chamberlain still believed that Hitler could be stopped without war. Now the democracies were better prepared, the Prime Minister felt, Hitler would be deterred. How wrong he was!

Analysis of British foreign policy

There was actually something of a contradiction at the heart of British foreign policy. Britain wanted to be left alone, undisturbed by continental Europe, to make secure the immense British Empire and develop British trade and prosperity. Britain wished to avoid alliances at all costs – they were a diplomatic liability – and adopted an increasingly isolationist outlook. However, at the same time, Britain was not prepared to abandon its influence and prestige and it felt it had a moral duty to intervene in world affairs, to put them right when it considered that it was necessary to do so.

Britain adopted what was essentially an ***ad hoc*** policy, that is to say Britain adopted a flexible and pragmatic approach to problems as they arose. Some problems were confronted; others ignored. This gave the impression that British policy was incoherent, indecisive and unpredictable. Now, of course, this generalisation does not necessarily apply across 20 years of

Ad hoc
A Latin term meaning for a specific purpose.

Key term

policy-making to each of the prime ministers and foreign secretaries involved, but there is some basis to it. As we have seen British policy was largely governed by three major concerns and, at the risk of some repetition, it is worth looking at them again:

- the revision of the Versailles Treaty to mollify Germany
- public opinion
- extensive global commitments and military and economic weakness.

Versailles

Many soon felt that the Versailles Treaty was too harsh and was storing up trouble for the future. We have already referred to Lloyd George's reservations about the treaty (see page 98). Most Liberals were opposed to the treaty and the **Fabian** Beatrice Webb denounced it as 'a harsh and brutal peace'. There was a groundswell for revision, and not just on the left. This, of course, was the basis for the deterioration of Anglo-French relations. Britain and France saw the treaty in completely different ways; for example, whereas Britain saw the League of Nations as a symbol and a forum for modifying the treaty, France saw it as the guardian of peace and security. Failure to reconcile Germany was commonly attributed to French rather than to German ill-will. Although reparations were swept away before the Nazis came to power, the feeling was that too little had been done.

Moreover, by the 1930s the notion of war guilt that had been applied to Germany gave way to the view that no one country had been responsible for the war, a view summed up in Lloyd George's observation: 'the nations, slithered over the brink into the seething cauldron of war'. This explains why Hitler's more aggressive approach was greeted by an acceleration of concessions, rather than resistance. Hitler's coming to power, it appeared, resulted from insufficient appeasement. Many in Britain felt that Hitler had a good case, and many were also won over by his anti-Communist stance and saw him as a useful barrier to Soviet expansion.

Public opinion

In the 1930s both MacDonald (prime minister 1929–35) and Baldwin (prime minister 1935–7) were primarily concerned with a narrow view of British problems, neatly summed up by the latter's biographer, G.M. Young, who commented that 'where France was thinking of her dead, Baldwin was thinking of our unemployed'. Baldwin was particularly concerned to respond to public opinion or, rather, had a shrewd eye for popularity and votes. For instance, in 1935 he created a Minister for League of Nations Affairs, despite private cabinet misgivings about the effectiveness of the League.

Indeed, public opinion was an important factor in the formation of British foreign policy. The memories of the horrors of trench warfare led to a 'never again' mentality summed up in the famous Oxford Union (university debating society) vote in

Key term

Fabian
A member of the Fabian Society, an organisation of socialists originally founded in 1884.

February 1933 'that this House would not fight for King and Country'. Public opposition to rearmament held the process back. In any event many felt it would only antagonise Hitler unnecessarily.

In addition, the need to respond to public opinion by supporting the League of Nations against Mussolini over Abyssinia had a disastrous effect on that policy as it neither stopped Mussolini nor retained his goodwill (see page 54).

Fear of the bomber was another pressure on government policy, encapsulated in Baldwin's dictum: 'the bomber will always get through'. The destruction of Guernica by German bombs in the Spanish Civil War made a deep impression on people, and Chamberlain saw for himself the vulnerability of London when he flew for the first time in 1938. But, of course, the truth was that the whole of the British Empire was vulnerable, as Chamberlain himself said: 'we are a very rich and very vulnerable Empire'.

Extensive international commitments

Britain's international commitments were summarised in a Foreign Office memorandum of 1926. Apart from obligations as a member of the League, and as a signatory to the Paris, Washington and Locarno treaties, there were commitments to Egypt, Abyssinia, to the Middle East, to Portugal, to the entire Commonwealth and Empire, which consisted of Australia and New Zealand as well as India and Singapore, large areas of Africa and the Caribbean and numerous places in between. It was an impossible task and the chiefs of staff finally stated as much in 1938.

Whereas Germany, Japan and Italy could focus their policies in distinct regions, Britain had to adopt a world-wide strategy. The real problem was that Britain simply did not possess the military or economic strength to defend such a far-flung Empire and could not assert itself when challenged. The army was thinly spread, everywhere weak, nowhere strong. The navy was still substantial, but had to take second place in the 1930s to the development of the RAF, which had to face the immediate threat of Nazi Germany. In these circumstances Japanese expansion in the Far East simply had to be allowed to take its course.

Few policy choices

All of this begs the question: what alternatives, what choices, did Britain have in foreign affairs when confronted with aggressive, expansionist dictatorships in the 1930s? The answer would seem to be precious few. Both the Treasury and the chiefs of staff supported appeasement and were happy with the Munich settlement. General Ironside stated: 'Chamberlain is of course right. We have not got the means of defending ourselves and he knows it. ... We cannot expose ourselves now to a German attack. We simply commit suicide if we do.'

Britain was not divided politically like France. The National Government had a large majority and the Labour Party, largely pacifist until 1936, but in favour of rearmament after that, did not create obstructive opposition. Accordingly, appeasement was not controversial until 1938. Up to that time Hitler asked for nothing that the British were not, in the end, willing to grant. Even Churchill did not complain about government inaction over the remilitarisation of the Rhineland in 1936 (and had approved cuts in the armed forces as Chancellor in the 1920s). But appeasement was not peace at any price, it was a policy of adjustment and accommodation, but accommodation that did not disturb British interests. The government was not prepared to give Germany a free hand in Eastern Europe, or the right to tear up the Versailles Treaty on its own terms. Thus, Chamberlain was 'hoping for the best [by appeasing Hitler] while preparing for the worst [by rearming]'.

Chamberlain's ambivalence

However, there was an almost infinite capacity for self-deception in Britain concerning the nature of the Nazi regime and the personality of its leader (although not in the case of Labour leaders Dalton and Bevin, and later Attlee). Chamberlain did not understand Hitler; he did not understand that his concessions generated contempt rather than gratitude. 'Our opponents are little worms. I saw them at Munich' was Hitler's summation. Limited, negotiated adjustments to the Versailles Treaty were not what Hitler wanted, but Chamberlain could not see that. Indeed throughout 1939 he continued to appease:

- the guarantee to Poland (see page 125) was more Halifax's doing
- Chamberlain kept Churchill out of the government for fear of antagonising Hitler
- Chamberlain did not make a serious attempt to negotiate with the Soviet leader, Stalin, for the same reason (as well as because of fundamental ideological reservations)
- Chamberlain was prepared to negotiate over Poland despite the guarantee
- Chamberlain was slow to react when Hitler invaded Poland on 1 September 1939.

Alternatives?

So, were there any alternatives to appeasement? Chamberlain could have had an alliance with France and possibly one with the Soviet Union. However, Churchill's alternative belligerent approach, some might say, was based on a romantic, unrealistic view of Britain's position in the world, and all-out rearmament would have had serious economic repercussions. Moreover, would Hitler have been deflected from his purpose? By waiting for a year after Munich, Britain was better prepared. The country was united, better armed and had the support of the Empire and the moral support of neutrals (although it had lost the support of the Czech army). Chamberlain was a decent man who had lost relatives in the slaughter of 1914–18 (including his best friend, his cousin, Norman) and did not want young men of the next generation to suffer the same fate. But he was up against a man who was quite prepared to risk another war and who placed his long-term goals ahead of all other considerations. Once again we return to the central point: Hitler caused the war. However, how far he was encouraged by Chamberlain's policy of appeasement and whether or not he could have been stopped earlier remains a lively topic of debate. To the historiography of appeasement we now turn.

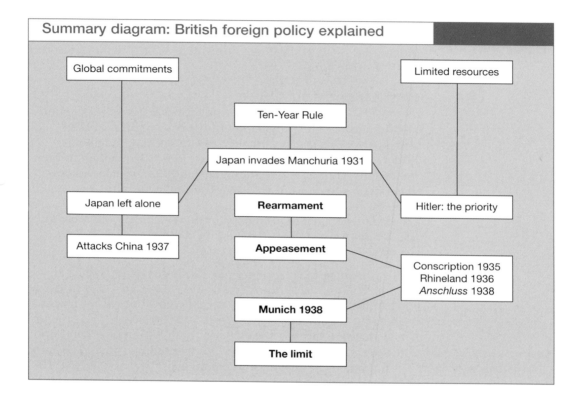

Summary diagram: British foreign policy explained

4 | Appeasement: The Debate

The debate over the rights and wrongs of the policy of appeasement has been one of the most controversial aspects of British historiography in the post-war years and it is a debate that is not over yet.

Key question
Has the historical debate led to a better understanding of appeasement?

Condemnation

After Britain's failure to stem the German invasion of France and retreat from Dunkirk in 1940, Michael Foot and two other journalists published a short book entitled *Guilty Men* that blamed the defeat on the politicians of the 1930s. It was their failure to stand up to Hitler that had brought matters to where they were in 1940. When in 1945 the full horror of the Nazi regime was revealed, this only served to further discredit those politicians who had tried to negotiate and compromise with the German dictator.

In 1948 Winston Churchill published the first volume of his Second World War memoirs, *The Gathering Storm*, in which he endorsed the judgements made by the authors of *Guilty Men*: 'there was never a war more easy to stop', it was an 'unnecessary war' brought about by the failure to stop Hitler rearming. Thus, there grew up the idea that there had been a series of 'lost opportunities' to stop Hitler:

- in 1936 over the Rhineland
- in 1938 over Czechoslovakia
- even in the summer of 1939 by the formation of an *entente* with Russia and France.

Churchill contended that Baldwin had failed to rearm because he feared electoral defeat and Chamberlain had been fooled by Hitler, who had pretended to want a settlement. Sir Lewis Namier was more blunt (1950): 'the appeasers aided Hitler's work'. It was Churchill's work that firmly discredited the policy of appeasement and created a historical consensus that lasted for a quarter of a century, reaching its apogee in Martin Gilbert and Richard Gott's indictment of Chamberlain, *The Appeasers*, in 1963. In this work the policy was characterised as dishonourable submission, the pursuit of peace at any price.

Revisionism

Yet within a few years **revisionism** had begun with D.C. Watts' article in the *Political Quarterly* (1965). Even before that A.J.P. Taylor had shaken everything up with his 1961 book *The Origins of the Second World War*; although controversial because of what he had to say about Hitler, what he had to say about Munich was equally provocative. Taylor described the settlement as 'a triumph for all that was best and most enlightened in British life; a triumph for those who had preached equal justice between peoples; a triumph for those who had courageously denounced the harshness and short-sightedness of Versailles'.

In 1966 Martin Gilbert drew back from his previous position in a new book entitled *The Roots of Appeasement*, which identified appeasement as the objective of British policy since 1919; however, he still condemned Chamberlain for continuing with the policy after 1937. Two years later Keith Robbins published a self-styled '**transitional book**', *Munich 1938*, which saw the settlement as 'the desire to avoid another war' rather than peace at any price.

What accelerated the pace of revisionism was the introduction of the **Thirty-Year Rule** in 1968, which made available the cabinet minutes and government papers of the 1930s. Now historians had a better picture of the context in which the politicians of the 1930s were operating and were able to appreciate both the complexities and constraints. In 1972 Correlli Barnett in *The Collapse of British Power* and Michael Howard in *The Continental Commitment* both highlighted the problems that Britain faced in defending its vast Empire in the 1930s. Barnett went further and stated that the Empire could only realistically be defended in war by turning to the USA for help, which is what happened.

Key terms

Revisionism
The process of re-examining existing interpretations, usually rejecting them.

Transitional book
This refers to the idea that a book went part-way to changing our view, by embracing a middle way between the old view and an emerging new view.

Thirty-Year Rule
Secret government documents are made available to the public after 30 years. So, in 1968 documents for 1938 were accessible.

Chamberlain rehabilitated

The rehabilitation of Chamberlain began in 1975 with the publication of Maurice Cowling's *The Impact of Hitler: British Politics and British Policy, 1933–1940*, which stressed the responsible nature of Chamberlain's policy; it was above all realistic about Britain's interests, commitments and resources. He went on to criticise Churchill for continuing the war against British interests after 1940, a position which had also been adopted by Barnett.

These works presaged the Chamberlain versus Churchill debate of the 1980s and 1990s. In 1979, G.C. Peden published *British Rearmament and the Treasury 1932–1939*, which argued that the concerns about the cost of rearmament and a long war were well founded, and in 1981 Paul Kennedy's *The Realities Behind Diplomacy* summarised historians' work on the domestic pressures which helped to shape appeasement policies. By the 1980s we were much more aware of the difficult strategic, economic and domestic context in which the politicians of the 1930s had been working.

The rehabilitation of Chamberlain continued in the early 1980s through the writings of David Dilks, although his major biography, *Neville Chamberlain, 1869–1929* (1984), has yet to reach the 1930s, as the title suggests. In 1989, John Charmley published what is perhaps the most complete defence of Chamberlain, *Chamberlain and the Lost Peace*. He followed this up with an attack on Churchill in *Churchill: The End of Glory* (1993) and completed the trilogy with *Churchill's Grand Alliance* (1995). Charmley's position is that appeasement was justified because war with Germany would be ruinous if Britain won or lost (as it turned out to be), and had Hitler been a normal statesman who would have been prepared to compromise and show patience, all would have been well. Thus, criticism should be confined to Hitler rather than Chamberlain. Moreover, Churchill's decision to fight on in 1940 handed world ascendancy to the USA, Eastern Europe to the Soviet Union and spelled the end of the British Empire.

The debate continues

However, Churchill has had his defenders and Chamberlain still has his critics. Richard Cockett in *Twilight of the Truth* (1989) demonstrated how Chamberlain manipulated the press to suppress opposition to his policy and Andrew Roberts in his 1991 biography of Lord Halifax demonstrated that it was the Foreign Secretary who was responsible for abandoning appeasement after Munich, as Chamberlain became an increasingly isolated figure. Indeed, R.A.C. Parker in *Chamberlain and Appeasement* (1993) made it clear that Chamberlain stuck to appeasement long after it was evident to almost everyone else that Hitler could not be trusted. However, Parker's central point, that there were alternatives to appeasement such as a military alliance with France and the Soviet Union, is only viable if we assume that Hitler could be stopped by it. If we accept that he was determined to gain *lebensraum* in the East regardless of any opposition, then war was bound to come sooner or later. All roads seem to lead back to Hitler.

Conclusion

As you can see, appeasement is clearly a highly complex issue and the historical debate is ongoing. While we now better understand why the policy was adopted, we cannot avoid the fact that it was a failure. It failed because Hitler had a programme of his own and he was not prepared to change course. It did, however, buy the democracies valuable time and there is no doubt that Chamberlain's motives were honourable, he wanted to save a generation of young men from slaughter, but his judgement of Hitler's personality and how events were unfolding was mistaken. Churchill told him after the Munich crisis that he had been given a choice between 'dishonour and war: you chose dishonour, but you will still have war' and he was proved right. Similarly, and earlier, in February 1938, Ernest Bevin, the trade union leader, stated:

> I have never believed from the first day when Hitler came to office but that he intended at the right moment and when he was strong enough, to wage war in the world. Neither do I believe, with that kind of philosophy that there is any possibility to arrive at agreements with Hitler and Mussolini.

Chamberlain may have been a poor judge of Hitler, but not everyone was; and as 1939 progressed more and more people came to see what he was really like.

Some key books in the debate

Correlli Barnett, *The Collapse of British Power* (Eyre Methuen, 1972).
John Charmley, *Chamberlain and the Lost Peace* (Hodder, 1989).
John Charmley, *Churchill: The End of Glory* (Hodder, 1993).
John Charmley, *Churchill's Grand Alliance* (Hodder, 1995).
Winston Churchill, *The Gathering Storm* (originally 1948, Penguin edn, 2005).
Richard Cockett, *Twilight of the Truth* (Weidenfeld & Nicolson, 1989).
Maurice Cowling, *The Impact of Hitler: British Politics and British Policy, 1933–1940* (CUP, 1975).
Martin Gilbert *The Roots of Appeasement* (originally 1966, New American library edn, 1970).
Martin Gilbert and Richard Gott, *The Appeasers* (originally 1963, Phoenix edn, 2002).
Michael Howard, *The Continental Commitment* (originally 1972, Prometheus edn, 1989).
R.A.C. Parker, *Chamberlain and Appeasement* (Macmillan, 1993).
Andrew Roberts, *The Holy Fox: A Biography of Lord Halifax* (Weidenfeld & Nicolson, 1991).
A.J.P. Taylor, *Origins of the Second World War* (Hamish Hamilton, 1961).

Study Guide: Advanced-level Questions
In the style of OCR
Study the following four passages A, B, C and D, about disarmament and the Ten-Year Rule, and answer the question which follows.

Passage A

From: A.J.P. Taylor, English History 1914–45, *published in 1965; an historian who argues that British disarmament up to 1932 made good sense.*

In 1919 Lloyd George told the service chiefs that they need not anticipate a major war within the next 10 years. In 1925 the service chiefs asked again and were given the same answer (an answer repeated in 1926 and 1927). In 1928 the service chiefs were told, on Churchill's prompting, that they need ask no more: the 10 year's freedom from major war began automatically each morning. The instruction was cancelled only in 1932. The Ten-Year Rule came in for much criticism later when it seemed that British disarmament had been carried on too long. Yet it was a sound political judgement when it started, and even its prolongation could be justified. There was not much point in maintaining great armaments when no conceivable enemy existed.

Passage B

From: R.R. James, Churchill: A Study in Failure, *published in 1970; a political historian who argues that the Ten-Year Rule had a disastrous impact on the defence of Britain.*

The long-term effects of the continued run down of the Services were considerable. When the Ten-Year Rule was cancelled in 1932 the armament factories had switched to other activities, or were so under-staffed that virtually the whole armament industry had to be rebuilt from scratch. The comment of Sir Warren Fisher, Permanent Secretary to the Treasury [and head of the civil service 1919–39, writing in 1948], may be quoted: 'We converted ourselves to military impotence. To have disarmed so drastically in the 2 or 3 years after the war was not unnatural, though possibly not wise. But our government of 1924 to 1929 had no excuse for further reducing our armed forces to a skeleton as by then it was known the Weimar Republic was reconstructing a disguised army on a formidable scale. This British government's tragic action formed, unfortunately, a model for subsequent governments.'

Passage C

From: M. Howard, The Continental Commitment, *published in 1972; a military historian who argues that the Ten-Year Rule had little effect on Britain's military strength.*

The Chancellor of the Exchequer, Winston Churchill, having spent 5 years at the Admiralty building up the Royal Navy, was now spending 5 years at the Treasury trying with equal enthusiasm to cut it down again. In this he was fortunately not successful; but he did persuade the Committee of Imperial Defence in July 1928 to lay down: 'as a standing assumption that at any given date there will be no war for 10 years from that date; and that this should be the rule unless or until it is decided to alter it'. This was the famous, or notorious, Ten-Year Rule in its final form. But it was accepted only subject to annual review and to its being 'the duty of any department or dominion government to ask for it to be reconsidered at any time'. Since it was abandoned within 4 years, the real damage that it did to the capabilities of the British Empire was less than has been generally supposed.

Passage D

From: M. Gilbert, Winston S. Churchill, Volume V: 1922–39, *published in 1976; an historian and Churchill's biographer, who argues that re-armament was never possible before the mid-1930s.*

In preparation for a Parliamentary delegation including Churchill in 1936, Baldwin turned to Hankey [Secretary to the Cabinet] for guidance. Hankey gave Baldwin material on Churchill's part in the evolution of the Ten-Year Rule to enable him 'to speak rather pointedly about it'.

Although Hankey sought to implicate Churchill in the Ten-Year Rule's deficiencies, he had also to stress the roles of the Labour government of 1929 and the National Government of 1931. It was, Hankey noted, 'not until 1932 that the Government cancelled it' but, he added: 'Even then it was extremely difficult to launch any considerable expenditure on armaments, first because the national crisis had brought the National Government into existence, with the revival of our finances as its main task; second, because the Disarmament Conference had agreed a temporary truce in armaments.'

Using these four passages and your own knowledge, assess the impact of the Ten-Year Rule on British military preparations between the world wars.

(45 marks)

Source: OCR, January 2002

Exam tips

The cross-references are intended to take you straight to the material that will help you to answer the question.

The four passages need to be read carefully: too many candidates do not do this.

The four different historians are writing roughly at the same time, but all have different views:

- A argues that the policy was sound
- B sees it as a disaster
- C suggests it was not as bad as has generally been supposed
- D seeks to explain why the policy went on longer than it should.

Clearly, you need to evaluate each of these interpretations in the light of your knowledge. You might argue that it was a policy that made sense in the 1920s, but was perhaps a little irresponsible in the more dangerous 1930s. Against this, however, you need to take account of the constraints imposed by both finance and public opinion (pages 103 and 107).

Good answers analyse all the passages, not necessarily in equal depth, and cross-reference them showing how they disagree or differ. Contextual knowledge should be integrated into the argument and related directly to views put forward in the passages. Better answers must include judgement on the various elements considered.

Study the following four passages A, B, C and D, about alternatives to the policy of appeasement in 1938–9, and answer the question which follows.

Passage A

From: Winston Churchill, a speech in the House of Commons on 14 March 1938 following the Anschluss *(union of Germany and Austria), in which he puts forward a distinct alternative to the government's policy of appeasement.*

If a number of states were assembled around Great Britain and France in a solemn treaty for mutual defence against aggression; if they had their forces assembled in what might be called a Grand Alliance; if they had their military arrangements concerted; if all this rested, as it can honourably rest, upon the Covenant of the League of Nations; if it were sustained, as it would be, by the moral approval of the world; and if it were done in 1938 – and believe me it may be the last chance there will be for doing it – then I say that you might, even now, prevent this approaching war.

Passage B

From: R.A.C. Parker, Chamberlain and Appeasement, *published in 1993. This historian argues that 1938–9 saw a political struggle between Churchill's and Chamberlain's policies towards Germany, with Chamberlain in 1939 having to adopt much of Churchill's policy.*

In 1938 and early 1939 there was a clearly stated alternative to the government's policy towards Germany. Where the government stressed reconciliation towards Hitler, Chamberlain's opponents preferred 'the language of the mailed fist'. They wanted military alliances to encircle Germany; alliances dressed up in the language of the League of Nations. Opposition to Chamberlainite appeasement was widely spread by September 1938. The almost complete agreement on policy towards Germany which had existed in 1936 was gone. An intense and well-matched political struggle replaced it. Chamberlain's opponents were superior to his supporters in talent and eloquence. On the other hand, they were dispersed and did not form a united campaign front. To add to Chamberlain's workmanlike debating skill and his careful preparation, the Prime Minister had the advantage of an obedient majority in the House of Commons. Chamberlain, however great his political assets, was compelled, after his meeting with Hitler at Godesberg, and still more after the German occupation of Prague, to accept in appearance much of the alternative policy pressed on his government.

Passage C

From: William Rock, British Appeasement in the 1930s, *published in 1977. This historian argues that Churchill's proposed 'Grand Alliance', devised in response to events of early 1938, received little immediate support mainly because of Churchill's reputation as a rebel.*

Churchill was not a determined opponent of appeasement before 1938, partly because its ultimate form and direction were ill-defined. In March 1938, after Eden's resignation and the shock of the Austrian *Anschluss*, he swiftly emerged as an outspoken critic of what he now believed was the sheer inadequacy of government policy. From then on, Churchill's outlook consisted of his proposal for a Grand Alliance and the belief that a continuation of appeasement would mean a series of surrenders until all of Britain's friends had been 'thrown to the wolves' and Britain was left to face its fate alone. But his long reputation as a Conservative party rebel, and an aggressive one at that, prevented his views from carrying full weight until the international situation had drastically deteriorated.

Passage D

From: John Charmley, Churchill: The End of Glory, *published in 1993. This historian argues that Churchill's 'Grand Alliance' remained unrealistic until its possible members were brought together by the demands of war.*

The 'Grand Alliance' was a wonderful slogan but it was not practical politics. Britain was not ready for war; nor were the French. In any case, neither of them was preparing for an offensive war. Russia, whom Churchill wanted to join the proposed Alliance, had recently purged her armed forces extensively. Moreover, Russia caused more problems than she solved as a member of the potential 'Alliance'. The Czechs, the Poles, the Rumanians all distrusted the Russians at least as much as they distrusted the Nazis. Then there remained the problem of the Americans. Churchill was always apt to become a slave of his own ideas and to assume that to coin a brilliant phrase was to solve a problem. However, the road to the 'Grand Alliance' was a long and a hard one. It came about only when dire necessity convinced its possible members that if they did not hang together they would each hang separately.

Using these four passages and your own knowledge, assess the view that, in 1938 and early 1939, there was no realistic alternative to the policy of appeasement of Germany. (45 marks)

Source: OCR, June 2004

Exam tips

What matters here is not the conclusion that candidates come to, but the quality and breadth of their discussion of the evidence. A sense of discussion needs to be evident and that needs to be related to the debate set out in the passages. This is the central question about appeasement.

The key word in the question is 'realistic', which may include several elements, including affordable, enforceable and acceptable (in this case, to the politicians, to the people and to the Dominions). The main alternatives to appeasement were a 'Grand Alliance' (the old balance of power in another form) and/or collective security; pacifism was never feasible. Appeasement is a relationship and to be workable it had to affect German policy. If the extreme *Mein Kampf* interpretation of Hitler is accepted then *no* policy was realistic in 1938–9. However, policy is never made on such a basis. The policy of appeasement was the only realistic policy because it was the one agreed by the governments of Britain and France. The alternatives were unrealistic because they had the support of only a few – and usually divided – opposition groups. On close examination, answering the question thus ideally requires consideration of 'counterfactual' history, but such an approach is *not* necessary. Of the four passages, A argues that the Grand Alliance was realistic; note, however, the number of times Churchill uses 'if'. Passages C and D argue that, in 1938–9, the Grand Alliance was not realistic. Candidates have plenty of opportunities to evaluate the passages by cross-reference and against their own knowledge.

Study the following four passages A, B, C and D, about the position and policies of Neville Chamberlain before and after the Munich Conference of October 1938, and answer the question which follows.

Passage A

From: minutes of the Cabinet meeting held on 3 October 1938. Chamberlain here is explaining his views on rearmament.

Ever since he had become Chancellor of the Exchequer in 1931, the Prime Minister had been oppressed with the sense that the burden of armaments might break our backs. This had been one of the factors which had led him to the view that it was necessary to try and resolve the causes which were responsible for the armaments race.

The Prime Minister thought that we were now in a more hopeful position and the contacts which had been established with the Dictator Powers had opened up the possibility that we might be able to reach some agreement with them which would stop the armaments race. It was clear, however, that it would be madness to stop rearming until we were convinced that other powers would act in the same way. That, however, was not the same thing as to say that we should at once embark on a great increase in our armaments programme.

Passage B

From: L.B. Namier, Diplomatic Prelude 1938–9, *published in 1948; an historian who comments critically on Chamberlain and his response to the Munich Agreement.*

When Chamberlain waved his 'treaty' with Hitler like a happy autograph hunter – 'Here is the paper which bears his name' – Europe was astounded. Could Chamberlain's trust, joy and triumph be genuine? His experience was that of a middle-class businessman and he infused into politics the atmosphere of the 'pleasant Sunday afternoon', dull and sober. He was shrewd, ignorant and self-opinionated and had the capacity to deceive himself as much as was required by his purpose and also deceive those who chose to be deceived. Once more he secured a great and miserable victory over Churchill. But within him there was an uneasy, unclear compromise which he preferred not to probe: if he was so happy about Munich, why re-arm? If he was playing for time, why make such a poor use of it?

Passage C

From: D. Watt, How War Came, *published in 1989; an historian who argues that Chamberlain's strategy towards Germany after Munich was based on a realistic view of Hitler and of Britain's diplomatic and military position at that time.*

Neville Chamberlain returned from Munich to the kind of triumph that even successful politicians can only dream of. Even he was carried away by it. The Anglo-German Agreement which he sprang on Hitler on September 30 was intended as a test. 'If he signs it and sticks to it, that will be fine,' he told his private secretary. 'But if he breaks it that will convince the Americans of the kind of man he is.' In the House of Commons on October 6 he asked that remarks made in the excitement of the moment should not be taken too literally. As the enthusiasms ebbed away, Chamberlain was left with two convictions. First, that the utmost must be done to exploit the Anglo-German Agreement and to build towards a European settlement. Second, that the circumstances which forced Munich on Britain must not be left unrepaired. The first demanded the taking up of contacts with Hitler and Mussolini. The second demanded that everything possible be done to strengthen France and to accelerate the process of British rearmament. It also demanded, though it took Halifax a long time to convince Chamberlain of this, a mending of the fences with Soviet Russia.

Passage D

From: F. McDonough, Neville Chamberlain. Appeasement and the British Road to War, *published in 1998; an historian who argues that, after Munich, Chamberlain remained committed to the policy of appeasement.*

It is important to examine what Chamberlain expected to flow from Munich. It seems that he believed that Hitler was anxious for British friendship. It is also equally apparent that Chamberlain had not lost faith in conciliation and diplomacy as the best weapons to prevent war. On 3 October, Chamberlain believed 'contacts with the Dictator Powers had opened up the possibility that we might be able to reach some agreement with them which would stop the armaments race'. On 31 October, Chamberlain told the Cabinet: 'Our foreign policy was one of appeasement', with the central aim of 'establishing relations with Dictator Powers which will lead to a settlement in Europe'. What Chamberlain wanted, above all, was 'more support for my policy and not a strengthening of those who don't believe in it'. He was not as harassed by doubts over appeasement as many of his colleagues.

Using these four passages and your own knowledge, explain why the Munich Agreement has caused so much controversy.

(45 marks)

Source: OCR, June 2002

Exam tips

Make sure you refer to all four documents, evaluate them and place them in context. It is also important somehow to divorce yourself from hindsight: we know the policy failed so it is tempting to just criticise. You need to try and see events from the viewpoint of contemporaries. Much of the criticism of Chamberlain reflects the disgust the war generation felt for the man who had tried to deal with someone who turned out to be so evil. However, he was greeted as a hero, initially.

- How moral was the agreement?
- Is pragmatism to be preferred to principle?
- How naïve was Chamberlain?
- How convinced was he that appeasement would work?
- How committed was he to rearmament?
- Did Munich save Britain by giving us time to set up the radar stations and build more aircraft?

6 The Outbreak of War

Key dates

1938	September 29	Munich Conference
1939	February 22	Britain agreed to prepare an army to be dispatched to the continent
	March 13–14	Invasion of Bohemia and Moravia
	March 30–31	Britain and France issued a guarantee to Poland
	April 3	Hitler ordered invasion plan of Poland
	April 7	Mussolini invaded Albania
	April 13	Britain and France issued guarantees to Greece and Romania
	May 22	Pact of Steel
	August 23	Nazi–Soviet Pact
	September 1	Hitler invaded Poland
	September 3	Britain and France declared war on Germany

1 | The European Diplomatic Situation Transformed, October 1938 to April 1939

Key question
What was Hitler's reaction to the Munich settlement?

One of the most ominous by-products of the Munich settlement was that it reinforced Hitler's reputation for infallibility, to himself as well as to those around him. As has already been indicated (see page 77), the *Führer* felt cheated by the settlement over

Key dates

Munich Conference:
29 September 1938

Britain agreed to
prepare an army
to be dispatched to
the continent:
22 February 1939

Czechoslovakia; in his final days in the bunker in 1945 he regretted not starting the war a year earlier over this issue, and he was probably jealous of the praise heaped on Chamberlain for saving the world from war. On 10 October he privately declared his intention of annexing what remained of Czechoslovakia and on 21 October approved a plan for its 'liquidation' (see page 82) as well as for 'taking possession of Memel,' a German city which had been taken by the Lithuanians after the war (see the map on page 12).

The rump of Czechoslovakia was now unstable and the regimes of both Slovakia and Ruthenia were given autonomy. When the Slovak Deputy Prime Minister, Durcansky, visited Berlin in October 1938, Göring encouraged him to press for Slovak independence, as indeed did Hitler when he met Slovak leaders the following February. Hitler's plan was to make Czechoslovakia break up from within.

Key question
What was Britain's
reaction to the
Munich settlement?

British misgivings

In the aftermath of the Munich settlement, Chamberlain still hoped for a general settlement and, on 6 November, a Franco-German declaration was signed along similar lines to the separate Anglo-German document that Chamberlain had so proudly displayed on his return from Munich (see page 81). However, the Nazi attack on Jews on the night of 9 November – known as 'Crystal Night' because of all the broken glass from ransacked shops – brought condemnation in the British press and led to another decisive shift in British public opinion, a shift that led eventually to the dramatic change in British policy which has already been referred to (see page 106).

In January 1939 the British government received a series of disturbing reports about German ambitions against Czechoslovakia, Memel and Poland which were finally taken seriously. The previous assumption, that Hitler's aims were limited, was now discarded. In addition, the joint planning sub-committee produced a much more favourable assessment of Britain's strategic position by emphasising that the German economy was too weak to sustain a long war and, under pressure from Halifax, the government finally took steps to resist Germany and support France (see page 106). French policy, which had been in limbo since Munich, could now finally take shape.

Key question
Why did Hitler
negotiate with
Poland?

Hitler negotiates with Poland

In the meantime, Hitler had been making attempts to turn Poland into a German satellite. He did not initially aim at partition or conquest because his main aim remained a showdown with Bolshevik Russia and the conquest of *lebensraum*. Hitler felt that because the Poles were anti-Communist and anti-Russian, joint action would be possible.

For many years he had suggested an anti-Soviet alliance, but the Poles thought better of it. After Munich, the Nazi regime stepped up the pace. On 24 October 1938 Ribbentrop put Germany's proposals for the recovery of Danzig (a German city under League of Nations control) and a road and rail link through the 'corridor' (see the map on page 12) to Joseph Lipski, the Polish ambassador, but met with little response. These proposals were repeated when Poland's Foreign Minister Beck visited Berlin on 5–6 January 1939, but again they met with an evasive response, despite Hitler's hint of Polish acquisitions in the Ukraine in the future. Ribbentrop then went to Warsaw on 26 January to press for a decision, but again without success. The Poles did not wish to become German puppets, nor did they wish to upset the Russians by joining the Anti-Comintern Pact. However, it would appear that these demands were a test of Polish willingness to act as a German satellite, and the Polish government's failure to commit to Hitler forced the German leader to alter his policy dramatically and consider Polish annihilation. But prior to that decision, the *Führer* was faced with the break-up of Czechoslovakia.

Bohemia and Moravia annexed

Although Hitler had been working for the destruction of Czechoslovakia, once again the timing of the occurrence was not of his own making and it took him by surprise. On 6 March, in an effort to re-create a measure of unity, President Hacha of Czechoslovakia dismissed the prime minister of Ruthenia and on 9 March the prime minister of Slovakia. Hitler acted quickly to arrange a declaration of Slovak independence and on 15 March agreed to receive President Hacha, only to tell him that the German army was taking over his country. After suffering a stroke, probably as a result of Hitler's tirade, Hacha signed a piece of paper handing Bohemia and Moravia over to Hitler, and on 16 March the two provinces were declared a **protectorate** of Germany (see the map on page 78). German troops and tanks were already there.

Shock in Britain

These events created a profound sense of shock in Britain since there could be no pretence any more about uniting Germans; the Czechs were definitely not German. It now seemed that Hitler's aims were unlimited. Initially, Chamberlain's reaction was lame, but on 17 March in a speech in Birmingham he was more combative, complaining of Hitler's broken promises, posing a series of rhetorical questions about the fate of other small states and ending by stating that Britain would not flinch from resisting a challenge. Clearly, the influence of Halifax was at work here, but Chamberlain felt the deception very personally. On 18 March he told the cabinet, 'no reliance could be placed on any of the assurances given by the Nazi leaders'. The message was clear: Hitler could not be trusted and German attempts to dominate Europe had to be resisted, but the next time since nothing could now be done about Czechoslovakia.

Key date

Invasion of Bohemia and Moravia: 13–14 March 1939

Key term

Protectorate A state that is controlled and protected by another.

Key question
Why did Chamberlain offer to 'guarantee' Poland?

Key date

Britain and France issue a guarantee to Poland: 30–31 March 1939

Guarantee to Poland

Hitler was not listening. On 19 March he requested that the Lithuanian government hand over Memel and 4 days later it did so. This also created alarm in Britain, where there was a fear that Poland might succumb to German influence, so on 27 March Halifax proposed that a guarantee be offered to Poland. However, the issue was not Poland. As Chamberlain himself put it, 'our object is to check and defeat Germany's attempt at world domination'. On 30 March the guarantee (to which France adhered) was offered and accepted at once by Poland, and on 31 March British policy, which had really changed over a month before, was finally made public. The prime minister announced in the House of Commons:

> in the event of any action which clearly threatened Polish independence, and which the Polish government accordingly considered it vital to resist with their national forces, His Majesty's Government would feel themselves bound at once to lend the Polish government all support in their power.

Although the wording left open the possibility of border changes, the guarantee was meant to act solely as a deterrent and little was done in the aftermath to give the agreement any substance. This probably sent the wrong signal to Hitler. After all, there was little Britain and France could do to give Poland direct assistance. In any event, the pledge to Poland had quite the opposite effect on Hitler. Instead of making him cautious and take a step back, it simply infuriated him and caused him to comment, 'I'll cook them a stew that they'll choke on.'

In retrospect, it is clear that Hitler's occupation of Prague and Memel was mistaken, but his impatience and the logic of his plans seem to have robbed him of caution; from now on he seemed unable to break his own momentum. Chamberlain, for his part, still hoped to keep the peace, but we should not underestimate the emotions of a disappointed man; even Churchill conceded that Chamberlain was a man who did not like to be cheated. If Chamberlain had misjudged Hitler, then it is also true to say that Hitler misjudged Chamberlain.

Aftermath of the guarantee

The 6 months between the Munich settlement and the Anglo-French guarantee to Poland had witnessed dramatic changes. A new European situation had taken shape. Britain and France had come together and were determined to stop Hitler dominating Europe. Hitler for his part was more determined than ever to press on with his plans for expansion. It seems that the only effect the deterrent had was the opposite to that intended; Hitler always reacted to any move to curb his plans with anger and even greater wilfulness.

On 1 April 1939, the day after Chamberlain had publicly announced the guarantee to Poland, Hitler demonstrated his anger with Britain in a speech at Wilhelmshaven for the

Key date

Hitler ordered invasion plan of Poland: 3 April 1939

launching of the battleship *Tirpitz*, by threatening to scrap the Anglo-German Naval Agreement. Two days later he ordered his Chief of Staff, Keitel, to draw up military preparations for an attack on Poland at any time from 1 September 1939. On 6 April negotiations with Poland were suddenly broken off. Operation White, as it was called, was ready by 11 April, although it is clear that the plan was to entail a limited war confined to the objective of Poland: Germany was not yet ready for a wider war.

More guarantees

The tension continued to rise: in early April Mussolini marched his army into Albania, choosing the right moment for maximum effect. *Il Duce* had been a little upset that Hitler had not informed him in advance of his occupation of Prague; there was an element of petulance in his response and an attempt to get even. However, to the Western democracies the action seemed to imply that the dictatorships were in some way co-ordinating their activities and immediately Britain and France issued guarantees to both Greece and Romania.

Hitler replies to Roosevelt

The following day the US President, Franklin D. Roosevelt, addressed a rather naïve letter to the dictators calling on them to agree not to attack 31 countries which he listed by name. This elicited from Hitler what was by all accounts one of his finest (and longest) speeches in which his protestations of innocence were proclaimed and his real intentions not at all. Addressing the *Reichstag* on 28 April he responded by citing all the countries the president had mentioned and, to the mirth of those present, he went through them one by one with a straight face, pointing out that he did not have any designs on Ireland or Syria or Persia or Turkey or Spain or Palestine, etc.; however, the real sting in the speech had come at the beginning with the denunciation of the 1934 Non-Aggression Pact with Poland (he did not name Poland in the list) and the 1935 Anglo-German Naval Agreement.

Key dates

Mussolini invaded Albania: 7 April 1939

Britain and France guaranteed Greece and Romania: 13 April 1939

Pact of Steel: 22 May 1939

Pact of Steel

The following month Hitler and Mussolini signed a full-blown military alliance: the so-called Pact of Steel (see page 64). Japan could not be persuaded to join what would be a triple alliance and Italy only reluctantly signed, fearing its somewhat open-ended commitment (see page 65). Hitler hoped this would keep Britain and France neutral, and it is true that *Il Duce* had been making noisy demands for the French territories of Tunis and Savoy. However, privately both Mussolini and his son-in-law the Foreign Minister, Count Ciano, made it very clear that Italy would not be ready for war for 3 or 4 years (although this was not stated in the alliance). Still, that did fit in with Hitler's long-term plans, as he expressed to his commanders the following day:

> It is not Danzig that is at stake. For us it is a matter of expanding our living space in the East and making food supplies secure and

also solving the problem of the Baltic States. ... If fate forces us into a showdown with the West it is good to possess a largish area in the East ... we are left with the decision: *to attack Poland at the first suitable opportunity*. ... There will be war ... [but] it must not come to a simultaneous showdown with the West [France and England]. If it is not definitely certain that a German–Polish conflict will not lead to war with the West [we] must strive for a short war. But the government must, however, also prepare for a war of from 10 to 15 years' duration. ... The *Führer* lays down that ... the armaments programme will be completed by 1943 or 1944.

It is clear that Hitler had decided on war with Poland even if it came to a showdown with England and France, although that is not what he wanted. And the destruction of Poland was his objective, not the recovery of lost territory. Throughout June and July detailed plans and military arrangements were put in train, while the German press resumed its anti-Polish campaign. However, the diplomatic focus now turned to the Soviet Union, as Stalin suddenly found himself courted by both sides.

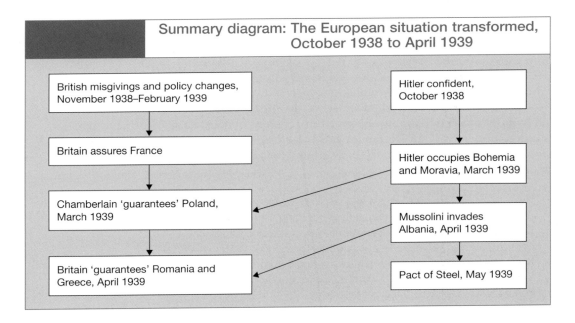

Summary diagram: The European situation transformed, October 1938 to April 1939

British misgivings and policy changes, November 1938–February 1939

Britain assures France

Chamberlain 'guarantees' Poland, March 1939

Britain 'guarantees' Romania and Greece, April 1939

Hitler confident, October 1938

Hitler occupies Bohemia and Moravia, March 1939

Mussolini invades Albania, April 1939

Pact of Steel, May 1939

Key question
To what extent was Soviet foreign policy contradictory?

2 | Soviet Foreign Policy

Ever since the Bolshevik revolution of 1917 and the establishment of the alternative Communist system, with all its international implications, the Soviet Union had been something of a pariah in Western eyes. It was not surprising that both the isolated Soviets and the defeated Germans should make common cause in the 1920s; however, with Hitler coming to power, everything had changed (see page 30). Stalin, who emerged as leader from the power struggle after Lenin's death in 1924, was above all a

pragmatist, and ideological considerations diminished in Soviet foreign policy in the 1930s, although there remained something of a dualism at the heart of Soviet policy: while the Foreign Ministry attempted to normalise relations with capitalist governments, the Comintern encouraged their revolutionary overthrow! Still, Stalin wished to avoid war at all costs, but the search for security was hampered by his personal caution and the Soviet Union's suspicion of all capitalist powers. Whether this seems a policy of keeping all options open or a policy of indecision depends on your perspective.

Pragmatist
A person who deals with matters with regard to their practical requirements or consequences.

Key term

Fascism

There were contradictions in Soviet policy, further exacerbated by the rise of the alternative ideology of Fascism. The Soviets found themselves caught between the alternatives of Nazi Germany and the Western democracies. So, on the one hand, there was the ideological policy of anti-Fascism, on the other, the expediency of peaceful coexistence with the Nazis; on the one hand, the hope of common cause with Britain and France, on the other the reality of those countries' appeasement of the Nazi regime.

The Soviets and *Mein Kampf*

Hitler's repudiation of Rapallo led the Soviet Central Committee to pass a resolution in favour of collective security in December 1933, although the door was always left open to reconciliation with Germany. Stalin said as much in a speech in January 1934. However, the Soviets took ideology seriously (the regime was after all built on ideology) and nowhere was the content of *Mein Kampf* studied more closely. In December 1933 Litvinov, the Foreign Secretary, stated in a speech to the Supreme Soviet in reference to Hitler and the Nazis:

> The founder of this party devoted a book to developing in detail his conception of German foreign policy. According to this Germany was not only to reconquer all the territories of which it had been deprived by the Versailles Treaty, not only to conquer lands where there was a German minority, but by fire and sword to cut a road for expansion to the East, which was not to stop at the Soviet frontier, and to enslave the Soviet peoples.

Similarly Premier Molotov also referred publicly to *Mein Kampf*'s policy of territorial conquest in his speeches to the Congress of Soviets in January 1935 and to the Supreme Soviet in January 1936.

Soviet options

Accordingly, in pursuit of collective security, the USSR joined the League of Nations in September 1934, and signed mutual assistance pacts with both France and Czechoslovakia in May 1935. Later that year the Seventh Congress of the Comintern proclaimed the new doctrine of the Popular Front against Fascism.

Socialism in one country
Socialism was meant to be a world-wide system, but when world revolution did not occur after 1917, Stalin decided it would be possible to build a socialist society in one country, i.e. the USSR.

Five-Year Plans
Production targets designed to modernise and develop the Soviet economy; the first plan began in 1928.

Cold War
The state of hostility without fighting that existed between the Soviet bloc and Western powers, beginning after the war in the 1940s and ending in 1990.

Profile: Joseph Stalin 1879–1953

1879	–	Born Joseph Dzhugashvili in Georgia
1894	–	Trained to be a priest
1899	–	Expelled from the seminary after becoming a socialist
1905	–	Attended a Bolshevik conference and met Lenin
1917	–	Bolsheviks seized power and Stalin became Commissar for Nationalities
1922	–	Became the General Secretary to the Central Committee
1924	–	Death of Lenin
1924–9	–	Outmanoeuvred opponents to become sole leader
1928	–	Announced first Five-Year Industrial Plan
1929	–	Announced collectivisation of agriculture
1934–9	–	Purged the Communist Party and army of alleged opponents
1939	–	Occupied half of Poland and attacked Finland
1940	–	War with Finland ended; Baltic states occupied
1941	–	Attacked by Hitler
1945	–	Hitler defeated; Eastern Europe occupied
1953	–	Died

Stalin was underestimated by his opponents and used both this and his position in the party to outsmart them: first allying with one group then another. He coined the phrase '**socialism in one country**' and attempted to make the USSR self-sufficient by a series of **Five-Year Plans**. He stated in a speech in 1931: 'We are 50 or a 100 years behind the advanced countries. We must make good this distance in 10 years. Either we do it or they will crush us.'

Stalin trusted no one and his paranoia led to mass executions and purges of both the party and the armed forces. His foreign policy was cautious and he surprised everyone by making a deal with Hitler in 1939, although he had little choice. He was true to the pact and said to Ribbentrop on 23 August 1939: 'The Soviet government takes the pact very seriously. I can guarantee on my word of honour that the Soviet Union would not betray its partner.'

When Hitler turned on Stalin in 1941, the latter was momentarily stunned. He recovered, refused to contemplate peace and eventually fought back, defeating the Germans, enlarging the Soviet Union and spreading communism throughout Eastern Europe. From 1945 he consolidated his hold on his satellite states behind an 'iron curtain', thus helping to create the **Cold War**. His paranoia contributed to its intensification.

Stalin was clearly one of the USSR's most successful rulers, but the kindly epithet 'Uncle Joe' belied his savage nature. When he became ill in 1953 his immediate entourage would not call a doctor as they feared another purge if he recovered. He died on 5 March of that year.

However, behind the public face of Soviet policy there was an alternative strategy characterised by confidential discussions with Germany about the possibility of improving relations. The Germans themselves made numerous offers of a substantial expansion of trade that the Soviets took seriously, while at the same time Moscow's policy of collective security foundered over the democracies' lack of enthusiasm.

Soviet dilemma

Basically the Soviets were fearful of German intentions, but at the same time deeply suspicious of Britain and France. Accordingly, Soviet policy seemed to be presented with two rather unattractive alternatives: to coexist with the unfriendly West or seek *détente* with the hostile Nazis. Clearly, the one undermined the other and the Soviets fell between two stools by pursuing both at the same time. While Litvinov was implacably opposed to the Nazi regime, Stalin, Molotov and the **Politburo** were more flexible and in April 1935 a trade credit agreement was signed with Germany and another in May 1936. Molotov's speech of January 1936, although it made reference to *Mein Kampf*, did not rule out the possibility of coexistence. However, 1936 saw Hitler occupy the Rhineland, give aid to Franco in the Spanish Civil War, launch a major anti-Communist propaganda campaign at Nuremberg in September and sign the Anti-Comintern Pact with Japan in November. The omens for coexistence did not look good, but then nor did the alternative.

Politburo
The principal policy-making committee of the Soviet government.

Key term

Failure of collective security

As we have suggested, in no other country was the threat of Hitler's ambitions taken more seriously, but the problem for Moscow was that the policy of collective security seemed to be going nowhere:

- France resisted Soviet efforts to transform the Franco-Soviet Pact into a real military alliance
- the League's failure over Abyssinia confirmed its impotence
- Anglo-French appeasement of Hitler made Moscow fear that the Western powers would be happy if Hitler turned against the Soviet Union.

Hence, Soviet policy was in a sort of limbo. In view of all this uncertainty, it made sense to keep all options open and in this context, in January 1937, the Politburo actually approved formal negotiations with Nazi Germany, but these came to nothing.

The Czech crisis

The year 1938 was dominated by the Czech crisis (see page 76). The *Anschluss* in March came as no surprise in Moscow and it was anticipated that Czechoslovakia would be next. From the beginning to the end of this crisis, the Soviets campaigned for international resistance to Hitler's designs on Czechoslovakia, urged the Czechs to stand firm and made it clear that they would honour the pact if France did. However, as early as May 1938,

A Soviet cartoon showing Daladier (left) and Chamberlain (right) as policemen directing Hitler and his henchmen towards the USSR and away from Western Europe.

when Litvinov met his French and British counterparts, Bonnet and Halifax, in Geneva, he came away with the distinct impression that Anglo-French support for the Czechs was very doubtful. In his speech in June he once again referred to Hitler's expansionist aims and continued to put pressure on London and Paris. However, Polish and Romanian opposition to the passage of Soviet troops across their territory, which was necessary to reach Czechoslovakia, made the possibility of an agreement unlikely.

Litvinov became certain that the Czechs would be betrayed, although briefly at the end of September, between Chamberlain's second and third visits to Hitler, war did seem a possibility (see page 80). The Soviets mobilised, but soon afterwards the Munich Conference took place and the Soviets (as well as the Czechs) were excluded. The snub felt by the Soviets at this exclusion and their mistrust of the democracies are well illustrated by the cartoon in which Daladier and Chamberlain are depicted as policemen directing Hitler towards the USSR.

Despite this setback, the USSR did not abandon its collective security policy and, after Hitler occupied Prague in March 1939, some form of collective action seemed a real possibility. In April 1939 the Soviets proposed a Soviet–British–French triple alliance, but now the Soviet aim was not only deterrence, but a firm military alliance to gain support in the event of war.

3 | The Nazi–Soviet Pact

German initiatives

Key question
How did Hitler and Stalin, arch-enemies for so long, come to sign an agreement?

From mid-1937 until the spring of 1939 little happened in Soviet–German relations. However, in 1939 Hitler's policy changed and Nazi Germany began its quest for a pact with the USSR in order to prevent a Soviet alliance with the democracies and to obtain Soviet neutrality in the event of a Polish–German war. The initiative did not come from Moscow. Since the collapse of the Soviet Union in 1991 more sources have become available and recent research has shown that Stalin's speech of March 1939 did not constitute a signal for reconciliation with Berlin. Similarly Litvinov's dismissal as Foreign Minister in May, hitherto seen as a significant gesture to the Nazis because he was Jewish, is also no longer seen in the same light. Soviet policy after these events did not change at all. They continued to pursue the democracies for an alliance. A more credible explanation of Litvinov's dismissal is Stalin's wish to assert greater control over foreign policy at a time when he believed the world was on the brink of war. Litvinov had frequently been at odds with the leadership; he was replaced by the more amenable Molotov.

The democracies' reluctance

Although German accounts depict the Soviets as being desperate for a deal with Berlin, Soviet accounts paint a very different picture. Germany's advances were rebuffed in May 1939 when Molotov spoke of the welcome prospect of a deal with the Western democracies. He rebuffed another approach at the end of June. After a lull the Germans made advances again at the end of July. This time Molotov was prepared to listen. Why? It appears he was becoming increasingly disillusioned by negotiations with Britain and France. In fact, he stated on 17 July, 'it seems nothing will come of these endless negotiations', and endless they were, a point so well brought out by A.J.P. Taylor in his book over 35 years ago:

> The diplomatic exchanges show that the delays came from the West and that the Soviet government answered with almost breathtaking speed. The British made their first tentative suggestions on 15 April; the Soviet counter proposal [for a triple alliance] came two days later, on 17 April. The British took three weeks before designing an answer on 9 May; the Soviet delay was then five days. The British took thirteen days; the Soviet government answered within twenty-four hours. The British next needed nine days; the Soviets two. Five more days for the British; one day for the Russians. Eight days on the British side; Soviet answer on the same day. British delay of six days; Soviet answer the same day. … If dates mean anything, the British were spinning things out, the Russians were anxious to conclude.

Moscow did not really know what to make of German advances; Soviet policy was indecisive and passive. Despite German pressure

Molotov remained non-committal. In any event the Anglo-French delegation finally arrived on 10 August to discuss a potential alliance. Criticisms of this mission are well known: the delegates went by ship rather than plane, the negotiators were of low rank and status, the British had no written powers to negotiate anything concrete, the French did, but had no powers to sign anything, and neither Britain nor France had any strategic and operational plans for a joint war against Germany. However, negotiations really broke down over the lack of Polish consent to the passage of Soviet forces across their territory.

Molotov and German proposals

Not until these negotiations came to a standstill did Molotov seriously entertain the German approaches. Already on 8 August the Germans had proposed an updating of Rapallo and made references to 'German Poland' and 'Russian Poland', words clearly designed to suggest that some form of territorial compensation at Poland's expense was on offer. By now Hitler had a timetable and was determined to attack Poland before the autumn rains. On 12 August Keitel, Hitler's Chief of Staff, was told to be prepared to attack on 26 August. The Germans were in a hurry.

With the collapse of the Anglo-French negotiations, the clear goal of Soviet foreign policy now became the avoidance of a war with Nazi Germany at all costs, but it appears that this was very much a last-minute decision. On 17 August, probably at Stalin's request, Molotov agreed that Ribbentrop, the German Foreign Minister, could come to Moscow on 26–27 August, but this did not fit in with Hitler's timetable. So on 21 August the German ambassador, Schulenburg, presented Molotov with an urgent personal message from Hitler to Stalin for an earlier visit. Two hours later Stalin replied personally that Ribbentrop could come on 23 August.

The pact signed

Key date

Nazi–Soviet Pact: 23 August 1939

After Ribbentrop's arrival it only took two meetings to reach agreement. The Nazi–Soviet Pact stunned the world; it was a most remarkable reversal of previously held ideological animosity. The agreement consisted of a non-aggression pact and a secret additional protocol, which stated:

1. In the event of a territorial and political rearrangement in the areas belonging to the Baltic states (Finland, Estonia, Latvia, Lithuania), the northern boundary of Lithuania shall represent the boundary of the spheres of influence of Germany and the USSR. …
2. In the event of a territorial rearrangement of the area belonging to the Polish state the spheres of influence of Germany and the USSR shall be bounded approximately by the line of the rivers Narew, Vistula and San.

David Low's cartoon published in the London *Evening Standard* in September 1939. The body of Poland lies between the two dictators whose prior animosity is sarcastically referred to by the insulting greetings.

An open-ended agreement

This pact has usually been misrepresented for, as Taylor pointed out many years ago, 'the pact was neither an alliance nor an agreement for the partition of Poland', i.e. the partition was not a guaranteed outcome: nothing was certain on 23 August 1939 except that the USSR would be neutral in the event of a German attack on Poland. When that would be, and what the outcome would be, was not altogether clear at the time. There was no discussion of any co-ordinated military action. In fact Ribbentrop actually had to tell the Soviets to occupy their 'sphere of interest' once war was under way! Poland collapsed so quickly that the Soviets were taken by surprise and were not in a position to move in until 17 September, over 2 weeks after hostilities began.

Conclusion

What then are we to make of Soviet foreign policy in the run-up to the Second World War? Its main characteristics appear to be caution, indecision and the ability to face in two different directions at once.

The problem for the USSR was that it was isolated, disliked by both the capitalist democracies and the Fascist dictatorships. Hitler represented a greater threat to the Soviets so it made sense to pursue a policy of collective security, but because this was never really achieved the door had to be left open to the Germans.

There is no doubt that behind the attitudes of Britain and France there lay a long-standing distrust of the Soviet Union and Bolshevism. Chamberlain, in particular, was vehemently anti-

Signing the pact.
A smiling Stalin looks
on as Molotov signs
the pact. Ribbentrop
stands on Stalin's
right.

Red Army
The name given to
the army of the
Soviet Union.

Decimated
Literally to have
one-tenth
destroyed, but
generally to have a
large proportion
destroyed.

Purges
Literally removal by
cleansing, but in
Stalin's regime the
killing of people
considered to be
enemies.

Communist. The Soviet Union remained isolated and could not
afford to provoke the Germans. This perhaps explains Stalin's
somewhat less than wholehearted support for the left in the
Spanish Civil War: he might not have wanted to antagonise
Hitler. Moreover, it should be remembered that the USSR was
undergoing rapid and necessary industrialisation. At the same
time, in the period 1937–8, the **Red Army** was more than
decimated by a series of military **purges** which swept away almost
all its senior staff and commanding officers. The reasons why
Stalin should do this at such a tense time are difficult to unravel.
Perhaps the purges were designed to create greater unity, but they
seem to reflect Stalin's personal paranoia and also developed a
momentum of their own. Weakening the army gave added
impetus to the desire to avoid war.

Ideally Stalin would have liked a deal with the democracies, or
so he is reported to have said on 7 September 1939:

We would have preferred an agreement with the so-called democratic countries, hence we entered negotiations with them, but Britain and France wanted us to be their hired hand … and without pay.

Stalin's only option?

In truth Britain and France could not enter into an alliance with the Soviet Union without alienating most of the states of Eastern Europe. And Poland, to whom Britain and France were committed, would not have an alliance with Stalin at any price. Britain and France offered the Soviet Union nothing except perhaps war, and possibly war on its own. Stalin wished to avoid a European war at all costs; he already had to face growing Japanese aggression in the east. He therefore had little choice. The pact was the Soviet Union's only policy option; it was all that was on offer and it offered the prospect of no war (and territorial expansion, although this was not fully appreciated at the time). It is surprising that so much criticism has been levelled at Stalin for taking what was not just the best deal, it was the only deal.

Once again, however, it was Hitler who was taking the initiative: it was Hitler's timetable, it was Hitler's deal. The Nazi–Soviet Pact was a decisive event on the road to war. The Anglo-French deterrent against Germany, feeble from the start, was now completely undermined. There could be no possibility of military action in support of Poland from the east. The way was open for a German attack on Poland.

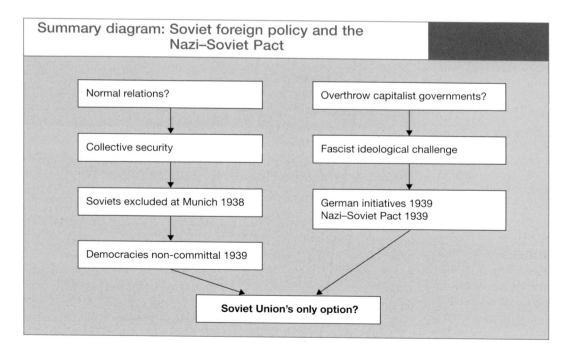

Summary diagram: Soviet foreign policy and the Nazi–Soviet Pact

- Normal relations?
  - Collective security
    - Soviets excluded at Munich 1938
      - Democracies non-committal 1939
- Overthrow capitalist governments?
  - Fascist ideological challenge
    - German initiatives 1939 Nazi–Soviet Pact 1939

Soviet Union's only option?

Key question
Why did Hitler's invasion of Poland lead to a general war?

4 | The Invasion of Poland and the Outbreak of War

Hitler's misunderstanding

With the pact, Hitler now felt that he was free to attack Poland: he did not believe Britain and France could do anything about it and he did not believe they would declare war. Indeed he stated to his generals on 22 August:

> England and France have undertaken obligations which neither is in a position to fulfil. There is no real rearmament in England, but only propaganda.

However, Chamberlain wrote to Hitler on the same day as the pact and stated quite categorically:

> Apparently the announcement of a German–Soviet Agreement is taken in some quarters in Berlin to indicate that intervention by Great Britain on behalf of Poland is no longer a contingency that need be reckoned with. No greater mistake could be made.

Hitler misunderstood British policy completely. Britain's real concern was not Poland, but Hitler himself. Still, he took comfort from those parts of Chamberlain's letter that reflected an obvious reluctance to go to war, and on 25 August he offered negotiations, and stressed his willingness to solve the tiresome problem of the Polish corridor, a problem which, in his words, 'must be solved'; which in reality left little scope for any meaningful discussion.

The attack postponed

Key date
Hitler invaded Poland: 1 September 1939

From Hitler's point of view, unlike the Sudetenland, this territory, the Polish corridor, had been German until it had been taken away by the flawed Treaty of Versailles: Germany's claim was a good one. Hitler was momentarily taken aback later that day when he heard that Britain and Poland had finally signed a full military alliance. He also learned of Italian reservations. Ciano believed Britain would go to war and Mussolini began to get cold feet. These two factors made Hitler postpone the attack on Poland until 1 September (a delay that actually gave him time to mobilise 25 additional divisions) and he went through the charade of negotiating with the Poles, although his self-styled 'generous offer' of discussions was never seriously intended and took the form of an **ultimatum**.

Key term
Ultimatum
Final demand, with the threat of hostile action if rejected.

Halifax and Chamberlain were still receptive to a diplomatic solution and Mussolini also tried his hand on 31 August, but Hitler would not be deterred. In fact he had been delighted when the Poles declined to negotiate (he felt this gave him a propaganda victory), and at 12.30 p.m. on 31 August he signed the Directive No. 1 for the Conduct of War. In the early morning of 1 September 1939 the German attack on Poland began. Hitler was determined to go to war (and, of course, Poland was determined to resist).

Britain and France declare war

There was a long delay between the German attack on Poland on 1 September and the British declaration of war 2 days later, and Chamberlain suffered some criticism in the House of Commons for being slow to send an ultimatum. However, it does appear that this was caused by trying to finalise **evacuation** and mobilisation plans and by trying to co-ordinate a response with the French. France too declared war on the same day, albeit 6 hours later.

Hitler was momentarily stunned by this (as late as 31 August Goebbels recorded in his diary that 'the *Führer* did not believe England will intervene'); it was neither the war he expected nor the one he wanted, and he seemed to be unhappy with Ribbentrop, who had constantly assured him that the democracies were bluffing. Still, he only had himself to blame; always the gambler, he had been prepared to take the risk of a general war. On 29 August Göring had pleaded with him not to play *va banque*, but Hitler had replied: 'throughout my life I have always played *va banque*'.

Hitler's miscalculation

So the Second World War broke out in September 1939 and, although it was the product of a long period of international crises, its immediate roots were Hitler's miscalculation that he could get his own way in Eastern Europe without a general war. He failed to realise that Britain and France viewed the Polish crisis in terms of their global concerns and great power status and he greatly underestimated allied military strength. Allied intelligence, on the other hand, was more realistic, the military balance was considered not unfavourable (two countries against one) and because the continued pace of allied rearmament would become economically impossible to sustain for any great length of time, it was felt that this was the best time to challenge Germany. By 1942, it was argued, Germany might be too powerful, which was Hitler's plan, of course.

Poland stands firm

Chamberlain hoped for a negotiated settlement to the last, and both the British and the French put pressure on the Poles in the final weeks of August to make some concessions. But the Poles would not be moved. So what we have at the beginning of September 1939 is the conjunction of these three elements that account for the outbreak of war:

- Hitler's mistaken belief that the democracies were weak and irresolute
- Britain and France's fears for their great power status
- Poland's determination to stand firm.

Hitler did not miscalculate in the sense that he did have a short victorious war with Poland and the democracies did absolutely nothing to stop him. He also chose the moment to attack them, and with some success, as we shall see in the next chapter.

Key date
Britain and France declared war on Germany: 3 September 1939

Key terms
Evacuation
The government policy of moving children from London to the countryside to avoid the dangers of bombing raids.

Va banque
An expression referring to gambling against the banker, i.e. against the odds.

A world war?

Accounts of the origins of the Second World War in Europe sometimes end in September 1939, but this is a mistake. For many historians the war did not become a world war until 1941 with the entry of Japan and the USA. But there is another reason for arguing that the real Second World War did not begin until 1941. If we consider that the war was caused by Hitler's ambitions, then his main ambition was to invade Russia, and only by following events down to that point in June 1941 can this argument be fully appreciated (the purpose of the next chapter). If we focus too much on September 1939, then the role of Poland and that of Britain and France loom too large and give an artificial picture. Only briefly did others seize the initiative; for the most part it was held by Hitler. September 1939, then, was only a stage, albeit an important one, on the road to a truly world war.

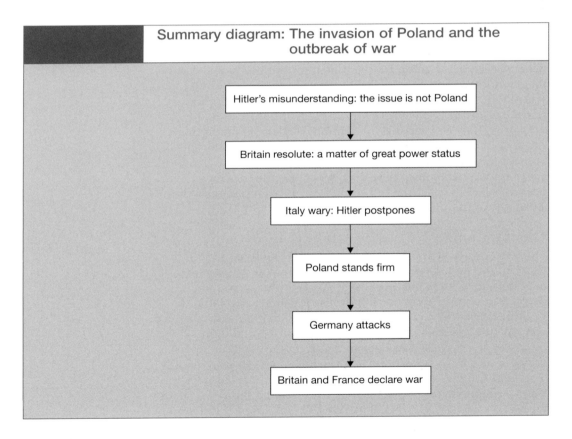

Summary diagram: The invasion of Poland and the outbreak of war

Hitler's misunderstanding: the issue is not Poland

↓

Britain resolute: a matter of great power status

↓

Italy wary: Hitler postpones

↓

Poland stands firm

↓

Germany attacks

↓

Britain and France declare war

5 | Conclusion: Could War Have Been Avoided?

Key question
Why did Britain and France go to war over Poland?

Could war have been avoided in 1939? The answer is yes, but it presupposes several unlikely events:

- One is that Hitler would have pulled back from the brink and would have been satisfied with his gains of 1938 – an unlikely scenario.
- Another is that the Poles would have simply rolled over and allowed the German leader to dismember their country as the Czechs had been forced to do – another unlikely scenario.
- And thirdly that Britain and France would have appeased again, looked the other way and allowed Hitler a free hand.

The democracies

Quite why Britain and France risked everything to stop Hitler in Eastern Europe is a topic of lively debate. After all, if the Western democracies went to war in 1939 to preserve their great power status, which they believed to be at risk, they surely lost it by doing so. Preserving the balance of power in Europe had always been an aim of British foreign policy, from the time of Louis XIV through Napoleon to the First World War. German domination of the continent would, it was felt, threaten Britain's great power status and, in the long term, represent a threat to the British Empire (especially since Germany was allied to the colonial predators, Italy and Japan). In addition, there is no doubt that there was a rising tide of national sentiment against Hitler in both Britain and France that made it easier for their governments to confront him; and it was the case that these countries had by 1939 the full support of their empires and the sympathy of the USA.

The right time?

Moreover, it was also considered a propitious moment both in terms of the improved readiness of their armed forces, and in terms of the military balance that it was believed could only deteriorate as time went on. British rearmament was geared to peak in 1939–40; by mid-1939 Britain could feel some measure of security (the radar air defence system was in operation, for instance), but because this balance could not be expected to last, the democracies were trapped in a timetable of their own making. The British military attaché in Berlin supplied reliable evidence that Germany would not be able to risk, let alone sustain, a major conflict for any length of time in 1939–40. Reports suggested that Germany would not be ready for any major conflict for a number of years, and we know this to be true. All Hitler's planning was geared to 1942–3.

The years 1939–40, then, were the only time the Allies thought they could confront Hitler with any reasonable chance of success; so they did. However, that does not make them responsible for the war. They wanted Hitler to back down, but he would not. The question then remains why Hitler was so determined to press on.

After all, this was the wrong time for him to undertake a major war.

Key question
Why was Hitler so determined to invade Poland?

Economic problems

There are a number of reasons why Hitler displayed mounting impatience and wilfulness from 1938 onwards. One factor was the economic problems raised by rearmament and his fear that others' rearmament would whittle away at his lead and make his position impossible by 1942–3. Hitler did not know that the democracies' rearmament programmes could not continue at the same rate, just as the democracies did not know that German rearmament was faltering.

Rearmament went forward in Germany in a rather haphazard way. After the 'May Crisis' of 1938 (see page 77) Hitler began construction of defensive fortifications in the west to meet the French threat. After Munich, he ordered a five-fold increase in the air force to meet any British threat and in January 1939 he approved the construction of 10 battleships (the 'Z Plan') to be ready by 1943–4 for a world war. The problem with all this was that Germany had neither the resources nor the manpower to keep up with this programme (in February 1939 it was estimated that there was already a shortage of a million workers). As Hitler himself said in August 1939 'our economic situation is such that we can only hold out for a few more years … we must act'.

Unco-ordinated policy

Moreover, Hitler was not at all systematic: he continually shifted priorities. He tended to encourage each of the service chiefs to press ahead with achieving his own goals, with little co-ordination and with little reference to what was actually possible. Because he felt he was under time pressure he began to telescope his programme, for instance, the expansion of the navy was given the go-ahead prior to the army securing the continental empire. The combination of a head start over the other powers with the lack of the means to expand production over the long term led to the idea that it was better to risk war now.

Key term
Blitzkrieg
Literally lightning war; an intense military campaign intended to bring about a swift victory.

It also led inevitably to the strategy of *blitzkrieg*, a short but decisive campaign of rapid movement, and to the idea of plundering the defeated countries to augment German resources (for instance, three armoured divisions in the French campaign were equipped with Czech vehicles). Of course, this argument – that Hitler was pushed into war by economic pressures – is that of the *structuralists* that was referred to in Chapter 1 (see page 4). Although it is an approach that has not been widely embraced by historians, it clearly has a basis in fact and cannot be dismissed entirely.

The wrong war

Germany, then, was only ready for the war of 1 September 1939, not that of 3 September. Only half of the army's 102 divisions were battle-ready and the navy was distinctly inferior to that of

Britain and even to that of France. Although the air force was strong, the Polish campaign used up a half of Germany's total ammunition stock and left it vulnerable (an attack from the west might well have been successful in the autumn of 1939). Hence *blitzkrieg* was the only option, but it was bound to fail if the war became protracted.

Hitler's self-belief

There are other reasons for Hitler's growing impatience in 1939:

- One was his increased sense of self-confidence, which had been fed by success after success: he felt he could turn his obsessions into reality by sheer willpower.
- Another reason was his desire to capitalise on public goodwill (there was no general desire for war in Germany in 1939 but the *Anschluss* and the occupation of Czechoslovakia had gone a long way towards restoring German pride).
- And yet another reason was his growing concern about his health that has already been referred to (see page 85), and even concerns about assassination. Indeed he himself stated on 22 August 1939:

> Essentially all depends upon me, upon my existence, because of my political talents. Furthermore, the fact [is] that no one will ever again have the confidence of the whole German people as I have. There will probably never again in the future be a man with more authority than I have. My existence is therefore a factor of great value. But I can be eliminated at any time by a criminal or a lunatic.

Hitler's ideology

The strength of Hitler's position in 1939 enabled him seriously to consider implementing his ideological aims. Once again his roots in the nineteenth-century racial philosophies of Social Darwinism and nationalism came to the fore as they had done when he wrote *Mein Kampf*. Hitler came to relish the prospect of a war, for him it was 'the ultimate goal of politics', its 'strongest and most classic manifestation'. Indeed, he believed peace was harmful and that struggle was everything. The world war, Hitler repeated, had never ended for him: on 23 November 1939, referring to the First World War, he stated, 'today the second act of this drama is being written'.

The connection between Hitler and both the 1914–18 war and the pre-war world is clear: eastern expansion had been the aim of the **Pan-German League** as early as 1894, as it was for Moltke, the Kaiser's Chief of Staff, 20 years later in 1914. However, we should not overplay the continuity between the First and Second World Wars in this sense, since Hitler had far more sweeping victories in mind and a new racial order brought about not by any natural process but by the murderous brutality of his homicidal anti-Semitism.

Pan-German League
An organisation set up in 1894 by Ernst Hasse to heighten German national consciousness, especially among German-speaking people outside Germany. Hasse called for German territorial expansion in Europe.

Key term

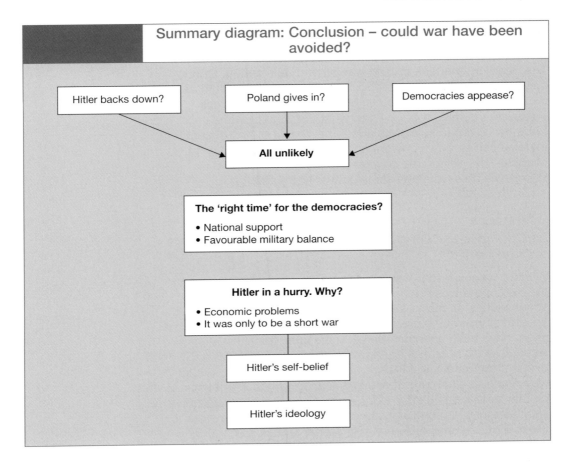

Summary diagram: Conclusion – could war have been avoided?

Study Guide: Advanced-level Questions

In the style of AQA

In this paper you are given one and a half hours to read the three sources and answer the three questions. You are advised to devote 45 minutes to question **(c)**.

Read the following source material and then answer the questions that follow.

Source A

Adapted from: F. McDonough, The Origins of the First and Second World Wars, *published in 1997.*

According to Soviet historians, writing before the collapse of the former Communist regime, Stalin's foreign policy attempted to uphold the principles of collective security against Hitler. Stalin reluctantly moved towards signing the Nazi–Soviet Pact because Britain and France deliberately appeased Hitler, undermined the League of Nations, and delayed signing a triple alliance in 1939 to deter Nazi Germany.

Source B

From Hitler's speech to his generals in August 1939.

The decision to attack Poland was arrived at in spring. Göring has demonstrated to us that his Four-Year Plan is a failure and that we are at the end of our strength if we do not achieve victory in a coming war. ... As to what the weak western European civilisation asserts about me, that is of no account; I experienced those poor worms Daladier and Chamberlain at Munich. They will be too cowardly to attack. ... The fate of Russia will be exactly the same as that of Poland.

Source C

Adapted from: R.J. Overy, The Origins of the Second World War, published in 1987.

Without Hitler's restless quest for empire, war might have been avoided. If the western powers had not been faced with an accumulation of crisis after crisis in central Europe, which built up almost irresistible pressure for conflict by 1939, German aims might have been accommodated in the international system without war. It must not be forgotten that war in 1939 was declared by Britain and France on Germany, and not the other way round. A large part of any explanation for the war must rest on this central point. Why did the two western powers go to war with Germany? Immediately the question is put this way round, the role of Germany assumes a new and very different perspective.

(a) **Use Source A and your own knowledge**
   How valid is the interpretation offered in this source by Soviet historians to explain why Stalin signed the Nazi–Soviet Pact?
   (10 marks)

(b) **Use Source B and your own knowledge**
   How useful is this source for an historian investigating Hitler's attitude to the prospect of war in 1939? (10 marks)

(c) **Use Sources A, B and C and your own knowledge**
   'In the years up to 1939, Germany deliberately provoked war in order to achieve European domination.' Assess the validity of this claim. (20 marks)

Source: AQA, June 2003

Exam tips

The cross-references are intended to take you straight to the material that will help you to answer the questions.

(a) It is insufficient simply to summarise the content of the extract and the interpretation it contains. You need to understand and evaluate interpretation in the source with reference to your knowledge of the long-drawn-out Anglo-Soviet negotiations and the narrowing options available to Stalin, who wished to avoid war at this time (page 136).

(b) 'How useful' requires you to comment on the strengths and limitations of the source: is Hitler overconfident? Is he trying to boost his generals' morale? Or does he believe what he is saying? What do you make of his denigrating remarks concerning the democracies? You also need to comment on his remarks about economic pressures (page 141).

(c) Clearly this question requires you to achieve a good balance between the sources and your own knowledge to achieve a sustained judgement appropriate to the full demands of the question. You will also need to show your historiographical understanding. Overy in C makes the important point that it was the democracies that declared war, whereas B suggests support for the question's proposition. Source A on the other hand demonstrates the importance of the Soviet Union in the equation. Candidates will need to evaluate Hitler's long-term goals – in *Mein Kampf*, the Hossbach Memorandum, the Four-Year Plan, etc., against his opportunism and improvisation. There is no doubt that Hitler did not expect a major war in 1939, but, on the other hand, he was quite prepared to take that risk.

Read the following source material and then answer the questions which follow.

Source A

Adapted from: A.J.P. Taylor, The Origins of the Second World War, *published in 1961.*

Whatever Hitler's long-term plans (and it is doubtful whether he had any), the mainspring of his immediate policy had been the destruction of Versailles. However, after March 1936 there was no more prestige to be squeezed out of attacking Versailles. The days of easy success were over. It was one thing to destroy the legal provisions of a peace treaty; quite another to destroy the independence of other countries, even small ones. Besides, it was never Hitler's method to take the initiative; he liked others to do his work for him. Things might have been different if Hitler had had an urgent, concrete grievance after the reoccupation of the Rhineland; but German grievances were, for the time being, in short supply.

Source B

From a statement by Hitler at a meeting with the League of Nations High Commissioner in Danzig in August 1939.

Everything I undertake is directed against the Russians; if the West is too stupid and blind to grasp this, then I shall be compelled to come to an agreement with the Russians, beat the West, and then, after their defeat, turn against the Soviet Union with all my forces. I need the Ukraine so they can't starve us out like in the last war.

Source C

From: P. Bell, The Origins of the Second World War in Europe, published in 1997.

For a long time, the tactics and methods of Nazi foreign policy contributed to its success, and enabled it to advance without war. Its potential opponents were baffled by methods far removed from the orthodox forms of European diplomacy. But eventually a revulsion set in [and] by 1939, Europe had come to the conclusion that Hitler and his Nazis simply could not be trusted. There was no point in negotiating with them; the only thing was to fight them and get rid of them. Thus it was that, while the aims of national socialism, if seriously meant, were almost bound to bring about a great war at some time, it was its methods that did much to decide when that war came about.

(a) **Use Source A and your own knowledge**
How valid is the interpretation of Hitler's foreign policy offered in this source? (10 marks)

(b) **Use Source B and your own knowledge**
How useful is this source for the historian investigating Hitler's aims and methods in foreign policy? (10 marks)

(c) **Use Sources A, B and C and your own knowledge**
'While the aims of national socialism … were almost bound to bring about a great war at some time, it was its methods that did much to decide when that war came about.' Assess the validity of this statement. (20 marks)

Source: AQA, June 2002

Exam tips

The cross-references are intended to take you straight to the material that will help you to answer the questions.

(a) Candidates need to be aware of the somewhat maverick approach that Taylor often takes to familiar material. Clearly candidates need to endorse those parts of Taylor's interpretation that are valid, but, equally to take issue with other contentions, in particular Taylor's provocative remark that Hitler may not have had any long-term goals.

(b) How much weight can be attached to Hitler's off-the-cuff remarks? Is he speaking for effect to conciliate the democracies after just signing the pact with Stalin, or is he simply telling the truth based upon his long-term goals laid out in *Mein Kampf*? Both the context of the remarks and some evaluation of Hitler's unpredictable nature are essential if you are to reach a balanced judgement.

(c) Considerable argument remains about Nazi aims and methods in foreign policy – about the degree of cold-blooded planning and/or Hitler's improvised opportunism and compulsive gambler's instinct. To score a high mark on this answer candidates will have to demonstrate a balance between the sources and their own knowledge as well as showing a historiographical understanding. Consequently, reference to the historians Bell and Taylor cited in the sources should be amplified by reference to other historians who have been studied. Good knowledge of Hitler's alleged long-term aims to be found in his writing and speeches needs to be balanced against a good knowledge of the events, and their improvised nature (page 83).

In the style of Edexcel

In the paper you are given an hour to write a single essay for which 60 marks are awarded. There will be a choice of two questions. Here are two examples:

(a) To what extent does Germany's increasing military strength explain Hitler's greater aggression from January 1938 to September 1939?

Source: Edexcel, January 2003

(b) Why did Hitler's decision to attack Poland lead to the outbreak of a general European war rather than to the limited conflict which he sought?

Source: Edexcel, January 2002

Exam tips

The cross-references are intended to take you straight to the material that will help you to answer the questions.

See Chapter 2 for some general advice on essay-writing skills.

(a) As far as the first question is concerned, clearly Germany's military strength was increasing, but Hitler's discussions about the prospect of a major war usually referred to 1942–3 as the time when Germany would be ready. Obviously, some discussion of military strength is essential, but remember that rearmament is relative: Britain was rearming too.

Apart from military strength you also need to consider other factors, such as:

- Was Hitler pushed into *Anschluss* and the occupation of Bohemia and Moravia (page 83) by circumstance?
- Did his success create some form of inherent momentum?
- Are his health considerations a factor (page 85)?
- Were economic pressures of great significance (page 141)?
- Did appeasement encourage him?

There is a myriad of factors to consider that explain Hitler's moves in this period and it may be artificial to single out one factor above another, but you do need to consider all the elements, evaluate them, weigh them up against each other and reach some sort of reasoned judgement.

(b) With regard to the second question clearly your focus has to be on Britain and France. Hitler felt his pact with the USSR would ensure that his attack on Poland would be a small-scale war, he felt the democracies were bluffing and was in fact quite shocked when they declared war. After all, he did have a better case for the return of Polish territory than he did over the Sudetenland which had never been part of Germany. So, why did Britain and France declare war?

- The issue was not just Poland.
- Why did British policy change even prior to Hitler's occupation of Bohemia and Moravia (page 106)?
- What was Chamberlain's purpose in issuing the guarantees (page 125)?
- Why were no measures taken to ensure the protection of Poland?
- Why did the Nazi–Soviet Pact fail to break the democracies' resolve?

When war was declared the German people were quite shocked; they had been so used to Hitler getting his way without war. You need to evaluate British policy carefully and be aware that not everyone in the cabinet was of like mind. Did Chamberlain believe that appeasement could still work, or were the economic pressures such that this was the best time to confront the German dictator? You will need to weigh up all these factors.

7 War

POINTS TO CONSIDER

This chapter deals with events from September 1939 to June 1941. You should consider why Hitler turned on the Soviet Union before he had defeated Britain and why he was so obsessed with the idea of an eastern campaign. The two main issues are:

- War in the west
- Barbarossa

Key dates

1939	October 5	Polish resistance ended
	November 30	USSR attacked Finland
1940	March 12	Soviet–Finish war ended
	April 9	Germany invaded Denmark and Norway
	May 10	Germany invaded Netherlands, Belgium and France
		Churchill replaced Chamberlain as British Prime Minister
	May 15	The Netherlands capitulated
	May 28	Belgium capitulated
	June 10	Italy declared war
	June 17–23	Soviets occupied the Baltic states
	June 22	France capitulated
	July 16	Plans for Operation Sea Lion drawn up
	July–October	Battle of Britain
	September 14	Italy invaded Egypt
	September 27	Tripartite Agreement signed
	October 28	Italy invaded Greece
	December 18	Operation Barbarossa finalised
1941	April 6	Germany invaded Yugoslavia and Greece
	June 22	Germany invaded the Soviet Union

1 | War in the West

The events of September 1939 to June 1941 may be briefly stated. The Germans won a rapid and overwhelming victory in Poland (fighting was over by early October) and, following a new partition deal with the Soviet Union, much of Poland was annexed (8 October) and the rest subjected to ruthless exploitation involving slave labour and racial extermination. Hitler set out to destroy the people and ultimately replace them with Germans.

France falls

In the west, Britain and France adopted an inactive and defensive role (often described as the '**phoney war**' although there were some attempts at economic warfare). In this sense, Britain and France did not really go to war at all in 1939. The guarantee to Poland had been a bluff and there was nothing the Allies could do to help.

Hitler on the other hand told his generals as early as 27 September that he intended an early attack in the west. On 18 October he approved Operation Yellow, the attack on France and the Low Countries. However, poor weather constantly postponed the action through the winter, which also led to what turned out to be crucial revisions in the plan.

In April 1940 Hitler attacked Denmark and Norway. This was a sideshow, a response to allied plans to cut off Swedish iron ore rather than a German initiative. The main attack in the west took place in May and it was an astonishing success: the Dutch were defeated in a week, the Belgians in 3 weeks, the French in 6 weeks. By the end of June it was all over. The speed of the victories took everyone by surprise, including the German High Command, the German government, and even Hitler himself. The opposing forces had been about roughly equal, but the Allies had been defeated by the superior skill, strategy and speed of their German opponents, which was just as well (from their point of view) because *blitzkrieg* (lightning war) was the only type of war that the Germans were really equipped for.

German policy in the west did not follow any preconceived blueprint and the rapidity of the victory caught Hitler out. He had no plans worked out, although there were elements of continuity with German aims in the First World War (drawn up in Bethmann Hollweg's September Programme of 1914 – see page 3). The army occupied the Low Countries (The Netherlands, Belgium, Luxemburg) and most of France, and the economies of these countries were placed under German control.

The Battle of Britain

Hitler did not know what to do about Britain. He expected the British to ask for peace terms and he was disappointed when he heard nothing. He finally made a vague appeal for peace on 19 July in which he stated: 'I can see no reason why this war should go on', but Britain did not respond. Over 2 months

Key question
To what extent was Hitler's success a complete surprise?

Key dates

Polish resistance ended: 5 October 1939

Germany invaded Denmark and Norway: 9 April 1940

Churchill replaced Chamberlain as Prime Minister: 10 May 1940

Germany invaded Netherlands, Belgium and France: 10 May 1940

The Netherlands capitulated: 15 May 1940

Belgium capitulated: 28 May 1940

France capitulated: 22 June 1940

Plans for Operation Sea Lion drawn up: 16 July 1940

Battle of Britain: July–October 1940

Key term

Phoney war
The period of comparative inaction between September 1939 and April 1940.

Key question
Was Hitler serious about invading Britain?

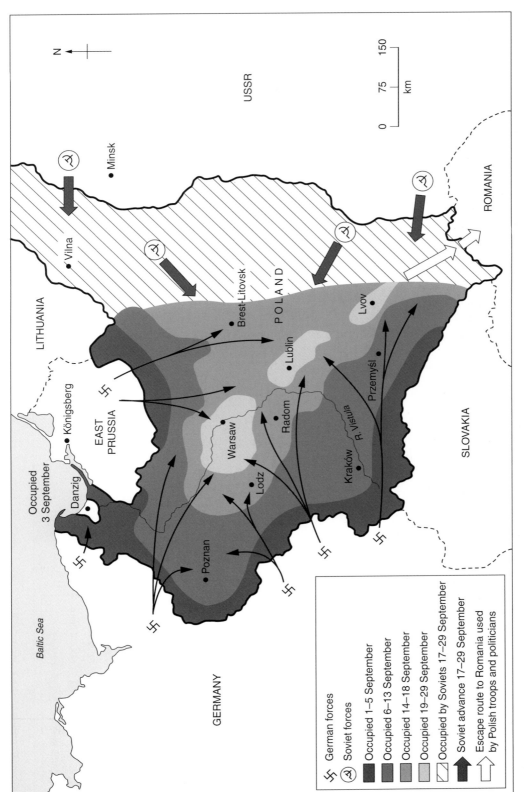

The German invasion of Poland in 1939.

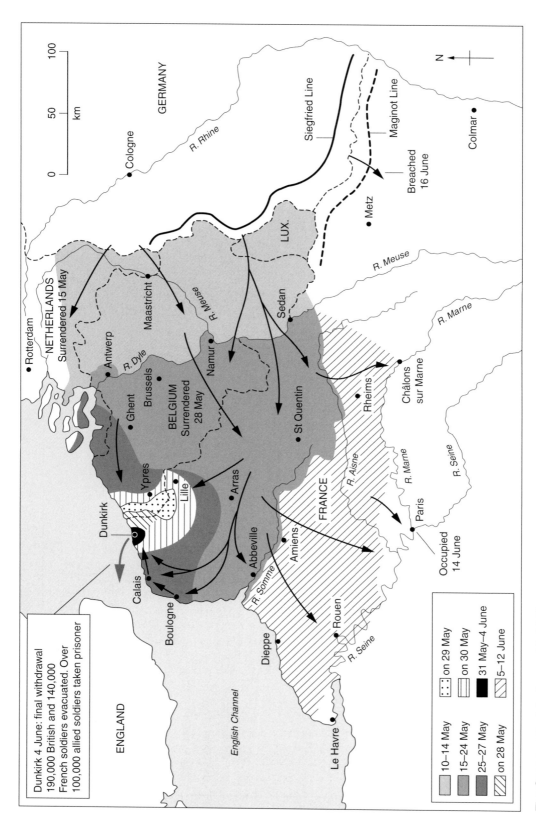

The German attack to the west in 1940.

Battle of Britain
A series of air battles fought over Britain (August–October 1940) in which the RAF successfully resisted raids by the numerically superior *Luftwaffe*.

Afrika Korps
German army force sent to North Africa under the command of General Rommel.

Italy declared war: 10 June 1940

Italy invaded Egypt: 14 September 1940

Tripartite Agreement signed: 27 September 1940

Italy invaded Greece: 28 October 1940

before, Chamberlain had been replaced by Winston Churchill as Prime Minister, and eventually he brought to British policy a dogged determination to resist, although many in the cabinet (especially Chamberlain and Halifax) were in favour of exploring the possibilities of a settlement.

Hitler ordered plans for an invasion of Britain (Operation Sea Lion), but these were always half-hearted, fraught with technical difficulties (German forces had not been built up for this task) and, once the *Luftwaffe* had failed to achieve air superiority in the **Battle of Britain**, were quietly dropped.

Alternative strategies

After the failure of the direct approach, Hitler toyed with the idea of an indirect approach against British interests in the Mediterranean (Mussolini had opened up this theatre by declaring war in June, invading Egypt in September and Greece in October), but Spain and Italy were not co-operative: Franco made impossible demands and the **Afrika Korps** was only formed and dispatched in February 1941 when the Italians got into trouble. Admiral Raeder's plan (of 26 September 1940) to strike at Gibraltar and the Suez Canal was not put into effect although a Tripartite Agreement between Italy, Germany and Japan, signed in September 1940, was designed to put further pressure on Britain to make peace. However, it made no difference to Churchill's resolve to keep fighting.

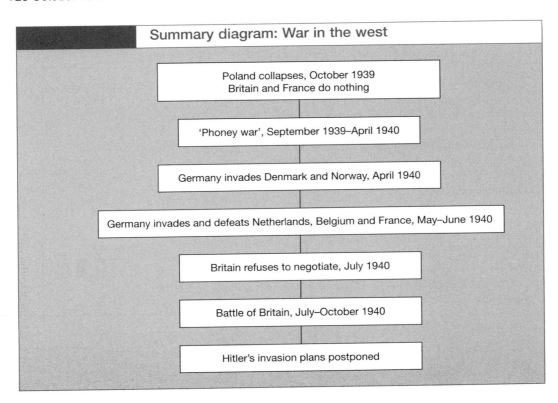

Summary diagram: War in the west

Poland collapses, October 1939
Britain and France do nothing

↓

'Phoney war', September 1939–April 1940

↓

Germany invades Denmark and Norway, April 1940

↓

Germany invades and defeats Netherlands, Belgium and France, May–June 1940

↓

Britain refuses to negotiate, July 1940

↓

Battle of Britain, July–October 1940

↓

Hitler's invasion plans postponed

2 | Barbarossa

Planning

In truth Hitler's thoughts had once again turned to what had always been his principal aim: an attack on the Soviet Union. As early as 2 July 1940 he told his generals that now his hands were free 'for his great and proper task: the conflict with Bolshevism'. Planning began in August and Operation Barbarossa was finalised in December.

This was Hitler's grand design; his ultimate goal. The scale of the military preparations and the time and energy devoted to them put Barbarossa in a different category to all Hitler's other operations. That it was his ultimate goal can be gleaned from all his writings and conversations with Nazi and service leaders over a long period, dating back to *Mein Kampf* (written in 1924).

Hitler had other plans, but he could drop them and, as has already been indicated, he could also be an opportunist, but he only took opportunities that appealed to him. For instance, the (very favourable) opportunities to strike at Britain in the Mediterranean and the Middle East in 1940 and 1941 did not interest him at all. The war with the Soviet Union was his principal aim and it was one of ideology and race: these factors also explain his ambivalence towards the British, whom he regarded as fellow **Aryans**.

Relations with the USSR

Of course, there were vacillations over the attack on the USSR, but generally speaking relations with the Soviets steadily deteriorated. Stalin himself had not stood idly by, he waged a not too successful war against Finland between November 1939 and March 1940, and in the summer of 1940, shocked and worried by Hitler's rapid victory in the west, he annexed the Baltic states.

After this, disagreements grew over Romania, Finland and Bulgaria, although this friction mainly came from Germany encroaching on the Soviet sphere of influence. Germany valued these countries' raw materials: Romania's oil, in particular. Yet economic relations between Germany and Russia remained good and the Soviets were scrupulous in their supply of oil and raw materials. Stalin did not want to upset Hitler.

Hitler met Molotov on 12 November 1940 and may have been prepared to postpone his grand design for a while, but the meeting convinced him that the Soviets would not accept German hegemony in Europe and that any kind of peaceful coexistence was impossible. Molotov outlined considerable Soviet territorial ambitions. Consequently Hitler did not respond to a subsequent set of Soviet demands and he stepped up the preparations for an all-out assault.

Key question
Was Barbarossa the culmination of all Hitler's aims and ambitions?

Key dates

Operation Barbarossa finalised: 18 December 1940

USSR attacked Finland: 30 November 1939

Soviet–Finish war ended: 12 March 1940

Soviets occupied Baltic states: 17–23 June 1940

Key term

Aryans
Caucasians (i.e. white) people not of Jewish descent.

Key dates

Germany invaded Yugoslavia and Greece: 6 April 1941

Germany invaded the Soviet Union: 22 June 1941

The Balkans and Britain

Hitler was diverted briefly from his task in April and May 1941 when German forces had to take over Yugoslavia and Greece after the Italians had once again got into difficulties. However, he would not be deflected from his main purpose, despite the Mediterranean opportunities after the capture of Crete and despite the fact that these excursions resulted in a 4-week delay in launching the assault on the USSR.

Hitler had decided to leave Britain in isolation while he destroyed the Soviet Union. He (justifiably) discounted the possibility of a British attack and he was not yet in a position to confront Britain on a global basis. Moreover, he felt that the conquest of the USSR would not only supply Germany with great economic resources and make it a truly world power, but also finally convince Britain of the impossibility of its position and bring it to the conference table.

The attack

The attack on the Soviet Union took place in June 1941. It was prepared over too long a time to be called opportunist. It was, in fact, as has already been indicated, the culmination of all Hitler's obsessions: the desire to conquer living space, to capture raw materials, and to destroy Jewish-Bolshevism (as he called it). Moreover, owing to the astonishing victories of 1940, the *Führer* was by now dangerously over-confident and he completely underestimated the scale of the Soviet Union and the resilience of its armed forces.

Arguably, then, this attack was the culmination of the whole process leading the continent of Europe into war and helps us put the events of 1935–9 in proper perspective. Of course, this is not the view of all historians. As has been suggested, some contend that Hitler was responding to economic pressures, still others that military expansion developed a momentum of its own and that the *Führer* constantly needed to reinforce his leadership and popularity with ever greater success. It can also be plausibly argued that the attack on the Soviet Union was brought about by a combination of Britain's unwillingness to make peace and Stalin's growing territorial ambitions.

A way of defeating Britain?

A statement in June 1940 after the collapse of France implies that Hitler had no immediate plans to invade the USSR: 'there still remains the conflict with the east. That, however, is a task which throws up world-wide problems … one might tackle it in 10 years' time, perhaps I shall leave it to my successor.' However, the following month British intransigence prompted him to remark: 'With Russia smashed, Britain's last hope would be shattered.' But a more effective way of bringing Britain to terms would have been to attack its interests in the Mediterranean and Middle East and, as we have already indicated, Hitler showed no interest in that strategy whatsoever. This thesis then, that Hitler only attacked the USSR to force Britain to make peace, is not convincing.

Russian ambitions

More convincing perhaps is the view that Soviet ambitions were the cause of the attack. Hitler's meeting with Molotov in November made him wary. After Finland and the Baltic states, would the Soviets expand into the Balkans? The USSR was expansionist and this could only lead to a clash. Yet we know that Stalin had no plans to attack Nazi Germany and in the final analysis we cannot ignore the well-documented fact that Hitler had his own reasons for attacking the Soviet Union. On balance we revert to his hatred of 'Jewish-Bolshevism' and his obsession with *lebensraum* as much more likely explanations. Indeed Hitler's relief at having made the decision to attack the USSR is palpable in this message to Mussolini on the morning of 21 June 1941:

> collaboration with the Soviet Union has ... been a heavy burden for me; for somehow it seemed to me a breach with my whole background, my views and my former obligations. I am happy to be rid of these spiritual torments.

At last Hitler was about to embark on an obsession that, fortunately for humanity, proved to be his **nemesis**.

Nemesis
Downfall, in the sense that it is deserved.

Key term

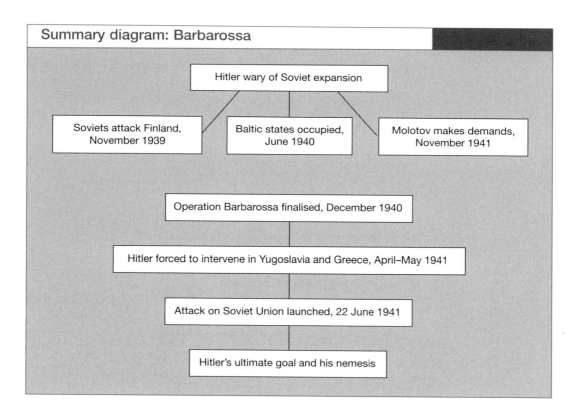

Summary diagram: Barbarossa

Hitler wary of Soviet expansion

Soviets attack Finland, November 1939

Baltic states occupied, June 1940

Molotov makes demands, November 1941

Operation Barbarossa finalised, December 1940

Hitler forced to intervene in Yugoslavia and Greece, April–May 1941

Attack on Soviet Union launched, 22 June 1941

Hitler's ultimate goal and his nemesis

8 Conclusion

POINTS TO CONSIDER
What were the causes of the Second World War?

- Was it due to a flawed peace settlement?
- An unstable international system?
- The economic collapse after 1929?
- The weakness of the Western democracies and their policy of appeasement?
- Or was it simply due to the aims and ambitions of one fanatical individual?

From the foregoing chapters it has probably been established that Britain did want war; France did not want war; the Soviet Union did not want war; even Mussolini did not want war when it broke out. Of course, Hitler himself did not want a major war in 1939, but it would be wrong to say he did not want war at all: he got the wrong war, that's all.

An Unstable International System

Key question
To what extent was the unstable international system the cause of the Second World War?

It would be too simple to ascribe the causes of the Second World War to just one man, since it was obviously the result of a wide variety of factors (of which Hitler was just one, but arguably the most important one). Undoubtedly the causes of the Second World War can be traced back to the consequences of the First. The collapse of four empires – German, Austrian, Russian and Ottoman – created a power vacuum in Central and Eastern Europe. Although Germany was beaten, it was not destroyed and undoubtedly possessed the potential power to revive and try to reverse the verdict. The disaffection of Germany together with the isolation of the Soviet Union and, more importantly, the isolation of what was arguably the world's most powerful nation, the USA, created an unstable international system policed by two old empires in decline: Britain and France. These two European imperialists were not really up to the job, although ultimately they were prepared to make a stand to preserve their great power status.

Hitler's Advantages

The Second World War can also be traced back to the consequences of the Great Depression that brought Hitler to power. Hitler was in fact operating in a very favourable climate. As has already been indicated the international system was very unstable and he possessed some distinct advantages, he did not have to pay reparations and he was confronted by a pair of pacific democracies weakened by the recent economic collapse. However, he also demonstrated great skill in exploiting the situation, in particular with regard to Britain's ambivalence over the Treaty of Versailles and also by exploiting the principle of national self-determination for all that it was worth. Hitler was very successful up to 1939, at which point he started to allow his ideological obsessions of race and space to regain the upper hand in his decision-making. But it can be argued this was what he had been aiming to do all along.

Key question
How important was the Great Depression in this equation?

Hitler's Aims

Even allowing for the context of a flawed peace agreement, unstable international system and economic collapse, it would seem that the war arose from Hitler's expansionist aims and the willingness of the other powers to allow this expansion to happen up to a point when it could only be stopped by war. The Germans built up an offensive army whereas the other powers did not. Hitler was out to dominate the continent. He could not be trusted to make a deal, therefore eventually he had to be confronted and defeated.

Hitler all along adhered to his major objective of acquiring 'Lebensraum in the east', although he was not committed to any specific policies for achieving it and throughout flexibility characterised his approach. That is why some historians have been able to dismiss the importance of *Mein Kampf*. But if *Mein Kampf* was not a blueprint, it certainly embodied his fundamental aims of race and space, aims he pursued with increasing fervour. Indeed as the war progressed, ideology became more and more important. In the later stages, for instance, his racial war against Jews seemed to take precedence over everything else as valuable rolling stock was used to transport Jews to the death camps instead of troops or weapons to war fronts.

Key question
To what extent was Hitler's ideology the main factor in causing the war?

Appeasement

If we take a sympathetic approach to appeasement, if we try to understand and explain British and French foreign policy, if we appreciate the difficulties their statesmen faced and their pacific intentions, then we cannot really blame them for the war, and we automatically revert to emphasising Hitler's responsibility once again. He alone wanted war. Of course, not all historians do take a sympathetic approach to appeasement. Some would suggest that the appeasers were guilty of wilful blindness, allowing Hitler too much and encouraging him to ask for more. However, yet others would argue that Hitler needed little encouragement because he had an agenda of his own.

Key question
How should we evaluate the policy of appeasement?

Hitler's Guilt

Whatever position one adopts on the origins of the Second World War, Hitler's centrality to the process cannot be denied, although he was not the only German who wanted to overthrow Versailles and reverse the verdict of the last war. The other Nazi leaders and the old imperial élite are not without blame, nor indeed are a large proportion of the German people: his foreign policy successes bound many of them to him. After all, he was only doing what the majority wanted him to do, exacting revenge for the humiliation and degradation many felt Germany had suffered since 1918. Indeed ordinary Germans came to develop a blind faith in his ability to do no wrong, to such an extent that he was able to lead them, like some pied piper, into a war in the east that the majority did not want. So whatever you decide, it remains a fact that Hitler attacked Poland, Hitler attacked Denmark and Norway; he attacked the Netherlands, Belgium, Luxemburg and France; he also attacked Yugoslavia and Greece and finally he attacked the USSR. No wonder the judges at the War Crimes Tribunal at Nuremberg did not have to agonise at length about where guilt lay.

Did the War Start in 1939 or 1941?

Key question
Did the real war begin in 1939 or 1941?

In a geographical sense there has always been some debate about whether the Second World War could rightfully be called a world war in 1939. Some suggest that initially it was just a European war (the European dimension has been the sole concern of this book), and that it did not become a world war until 1941 when Germany attacked the Soviet Union and the Japanese attacked the USA. Against this, it can be argued that Britain and France were global powers with global concerns and allies around the globe, which gave the conflict a 'world dimension' from the very beginning. Moreover, the adhesion of Italy in 1940 spread the fighting to Africa and the Middle East, which was clearly another indication of its global nature.

And yet it does remain true to say that the war was clearly only a contest for European hegemony until 1941, which was, in any event, Hitler's fundamental aim (although he felt that control of the continent would give him 'world power' status). But 1941 is an important date for another reason since it was not until Hitler attacked the USSR in that year that his true ideological purpose was fully revealed. As he said just prior to the pact with Stalin on 11 August 1939 in a revealing statement to Carl Burckhardt, the League of Nations Commissioner in Danzig:

Key term

Counterfactual speculation
Theorising about what might have happened had the 'facts' been different.

> Everything I undertake is directed against the Russians; if the West is too stupid and blind to grasp this, then I shall be compelled to come to an agreement with the Russians, beat the West, and then after their defeat turn against the Soviet Union with all my forces.

And that is just what he did do. It would be fair to say that **counterfactual speculation** has little real validity in general, but it could plausibly be argued in this case that if Hitler had not existed, then the Second World War might never have happened. But he did; and it did.

Some key books in the debate
P.M.H. Bell, *The Origins of the Second World War in Europe* (Longman, 1997).
Andrew J. Crozier, *The Causes of the Second World War* (Blackwell, 1997).
Ian Kershaw, *Hitler 1889–1936: Hubris* (Allen Lane, 1998).
Ian Kershaw, *Hitler 1936–1945: Nemesis* (Allen Lane, 2000).
J. Noakes and G. Pridham, *Nazism 1919–1945, Volume 3: Foreign Policy, War and Racial Extermination* (University of Exeter Press, 1988).
R.J. Overy, *The Origins of the Second World War* (Longman, 1998).
William L. Shirer, *The Rise and Fall of the Third Reich* (Secker & Warburg, 1960).
A.J.P. Taylor, *Origins of the Second World War* (Penguin edn, 1964).

Glossary

25-Point Programme   This was the Nazi Party's first manifesto and contained a series of aims.

Accord   Agreement.

Act of statesmanship   A skilful and mature act.

Ad hoc   A Latin term meaning for a specific purpose.

Adjutant   An officer who assists superior officers with communicating orders, correspondence, etc.

Afrika Korps   German army force sent to North Africa under the command of General Rommel.

Allies   Britain, France, the USA and those on their side.

Alsace-Lorraine   French territory annexed by Germany in 1871.

Amoral   Having no moral principles at all.

Anschluss   German for 'joining'. Annexation – to incorporate or add territory to one's own.

Anti-Comintern Pact   Originally an agreement between Germany and Japan signed in 1936 which stated both countries' hostility to international communism.

Anti-Semitic laws   A series of laws were passed in Italy discriminating against the Jews in the years 1938–9.

Anti-Semitism   Hostility or prejudice against Jews.

Apogee   The highest point.

Appeasement   Pacification; in this context the policy of conciliating a potential aggressor by making concessions.

Armistice   An agreement to stop fighting temporarily.

Army indoctrination courses   In this context, right-wing political courses designed to train ex-soldiers to seek out and expose socialist activity.

Aryans   Caucasians (i.e. white) people not of Jewish descent.

Autonomy   The right of self-government.

Balearics   Collective noun for the islands of Majorca, Minorca and Ibiza.

Balkans   The countries that occupy the peninsula in south-eastern Europe bound by the Adriatic and Ionian Seas in the west, by the Aegean in the east, and the Mediterranean in the south, i.e. Greece, Albania, Yugoslavia, Bulgaria, Romania and Turkey.

Battle of Britain   A series of air battles fought over Britain (July–October 1940) in which the RAF successfully resisted raids by the numerically superior *Luftwaffe*.

Bilateral   Affecting or between two parties.

Blitzkrieg   Literally lightning war; an intense military campaign intended to bring about a swift victory.

Blockade   The surrounding or blocking of a place, especially a port, by an enemy to prevent entry and exit of supplies, etc.

Blueprint   A detailed plan, especially in the early stages of a project or idea.

Bolsheviks   Members of the Russian Communist Party; the rulers of the Soviet Union.

Brenner Pass   An Alpine pass on the Austro-Italian border.

Capitalism   An economic system in which the production and distribution of goods depends on invested private capital and profit-making.

Cession   The giving up of rights, property, territory, etc.

Coalition   Temporary alliance of political parties to form a government.

Cold War   The state of hostility without fighting that existed between the Soviet bloc and Western powers, beginning after the war in the 1940s and ending in 1990.

Collective security   The idea that all the powers would band together against an aggressor.

Communism   A political theory derived from Marxism advocating a society in which all property is publicly owned and each person is paid and works according to his or her needs and abilities.

Concert diplomacy   A process or method whereby general agreement of all the major powers is reached.

Confirmatory plebiscite   A vote to approve what has been done.

Congress   The US parliament consisting of an upper house (the Senate) and a lower house (the House of Representatives).

Conscription   Compulsory enlistment for military service; forbidden by the Treaty of Versailles.

Contingency   Something that may happen.

Counterfactual speculation   Theorising about what might have happened had the 'facts' been different.

Craven acquiescence   Giving in, in a cowardly fashion.

Dawes Plan   Revised reparation payment plan drawn up by Charles Dawes, the US Vice-President in 1924.

Decimated   Literally to have one-tenth destroyed, but generally to have a large proportion destroyed.

Defence Law   By this law Dr Schacht, the Minister of Finance, was given authority to 'direct the economic preparations for war'.

Deficit financing   A means of conducting the economy in which government spends more money than it receives as revenue by borrowing in order to stimulate growth.

Demographic   Relating to population level.

Détente   An easing of strained relations, reconciliation.

Determinism   The belief that everything is preordained.

Deterrent   Something that puts someone off from doing something.

Diktat   A categorical statement or decree, especially terms imposed by a victor after a war: a dictated peace.

Diplomatic coup   A successful move in international relations.

Disarmament Conference   The Disarmament Commission had been set up under the auspices of the League of Nations (indeed it had been one of Wilson's 14 Points) to bring about general disarmament, or at least a reduction in armaments. However, it did not meet until 1932 and was short lived.

Divisions   Groups of army brigades, each numbering about 10,000–15,000 men.

Dominions   In the context of the Empire, the (white) self-governing territories with the same head of state.

Emasculation   To deprive of force, weaken.

Enabling Act (1933)   Enabled Hitler to operate as a dictator for 4 years without recourse to Parliament (*Reichstag*).

Evacuation   The government policy of moving children from London to the countryside to avoid the dangers of bombing raids.

Evolutionary approach   Referring to Hitler being prepared to take a slow approach in the belief that over time events would develop in his favour.

Expeditionary Force   A mobile army to be sent to the European continent.

Fabian   A member of the Fabian Society, an organisation of socialists originally founded in 1884.

Fait accompli   A French phrase meaning a thing already done and not reversible.

Fascist   'Fascism' derives from the Latin *fasces*, which were a bundle of rods carried as a symbol of power in ancient Rome; accordingly, the Fascist Party, which Mussolini founded in 1919, was authoritarian, nationalist and right wing.

Fatalism   Submission to what ever happens, believing it to be inevitable.

Five-Year Plans   Production targets designed to modernise and develop the Soviet economy; the first plan began in 1928.

Führer   The German word for leader.

Functionalists/structuralists   Two alternative terms for the same group of historians who believe that it was the structure of the state that created policy rather than a single man.

Gestapo   Short for *Geheime Staatspolizei*: secret state police.

GNP   The total value of goods produced and services provided in a country in a year plus the total of net income from abroad in the same period.

Government bond   A means of raising money: a certificate issued by a government promising to repay borrowed money at a fixed rate of interest at a specified time.

Great Depression   The severe economic depression of 1929–34 that most historians suggest began with the Wall Street Crash.

Hegemony   Leadership especially by one country.

Hoare–Laval Plan   Sir Samuel Hoare, British Foreign Secretary, and Pierre Laval, French Foreign Secretary, drew up a secret deal whereby Italy would be given about two-thirds of Abyssinia.

Hossbach Memorandum   The record of a meeting that took place in 1937 in which Hitler outlined his future plans for territorial acquisition and war.

Hyperinflation   Excessive price increases and a corresponding fall in the value of money. In the case of Germany in 1923 the government printed large amounts of banknotes which very rapidly became worthless.

Hypothesis   A supposition, not necessarily a truth.

Idealism   The practice of pursuing things in a perfect way, or trying to reach a very high standard, which can be unrealistic, as some ideas can exist in the mind but not in reality.

Ideologue   A theorist, one who believes in a particular system of ideas or rather a doctrinaire adherent of an ideology.

Il Duce   'The leader', as Mussolini was known.

Intentionalists   Historians who believe that it was Hitler's intention to wage war.

Interior Minister   Minister responsible for internal security with control of the police.

Irredentist   Literally, unredeemed, used in reference to the return of territory lost to France.

Isolationist   A reference to US policy that involved non-participation in or withdrawal from international affairs.

Jeremiahs   Doleful or pessimistic people; dismal prophets (from a biblical figure).

Lateran Accords   A treaty signed in 1929 between Mussolini and Pope Pius XI recognising the Vatican as a sovereign state.

League of Nations   An association of countries established in 1919 by the Treaty of Versailles to promote international co-operation and achieve international peace and security.

Lebensraum   'Living space': this refers to Hitler's desire for land in the east.

Little *Entente* So-called because it was an agreement (*entente*) with a small number of minor powers – Czechoslovakia, Yugoslavia and Romania – signed in 1922.

Luftwaffe Literally 'air weapon'; German for air force.

Maginot Line A line of defensive fortifications along France's north-eastern border from Switzerland to Luxemburg named after the French War Minister, André Maginot. It was completed in the late 1930s, but easily outflanked in 1940.

Mandates Territories administered on behalf of the League of Nations.

Matériel Available means, especially materials and equipment in warfare.

'Mutilated' peace of 1919 Although allied to Austria and Germany in the First World War, Italy had joined in on the side of Britain and France by the Treaty of London in 1915. In this treaty Italy was made a number of promises that it would gain territory in the Balkans and colonies. However, Italy received very little in 1919.

National Service Conscription; compulsory enlistment for military service.

Nationalism Patriotic feeling, which can take an extreme form.

Nazi Nazi is simply an abbreviation of the German for 'National Socialist German Workers' Party'.

Nazi–Soviet Pact An agreement between Germany and the USSR that contained a secret deal to partition Poland.

Nemesis Downfall, in the sense that it is deserved.

Neutrality Not supporting either side in a conflict.

Non-Aggression Pact An agreement not to go to war with each other.

Non-belligerence Literally, not waging war.

Nuremberg Rally From the late 1920s the Nazi Party held annual political rallies in the city.

Nuremberg Trials Nuremberg was the scene of war trials in which a number of leading Nazis were tried by a military tribunal between 1945 and 1949.

OKW *Oberkommando der Wermacht*: High Command of the Armed Forces.

Operation Barbarossa Hitler's invasion of the Soviet Union in the summer of 1941.

Pacifism The belief that war and violence are morally unjustified.

Pact of Steel A full military alliance between Germany and Italy signed in 1939.

Pan-German League An organisation set up in 1894 by Ernst Hasse to heighten German national consciousness, especially among German-speaking people outside Germany. Hasse called for German territorial expansion in Europe.

Paper tiger An apparently threatening, but in reality an ineffectual person or thing.

Pejorative A word depreciated in value, a word used disparagingly.

Phoney war The period of comparative inaction between September 1939 and April 1940.

Plebiscite The direct vote of all the electors of a state.

Politburo The principal policy-making committee of the Soviet government.

Political Testament Hitler's last will and testament which was drawn up in the bunker in Berlin in April 1945 when the Soviets were closing in.

Popular Front An alliance of French Communist, radical and socialist elements.

Pragmatism The practice of dealing with matters in a way that seems practical and realistic, instead of following any preconceived theory.

Pragmatist A person who deals with matters with regard to their practical requirements or consequences.

Principle of national self-determination The idea that people of the same linguistic, racial and cultural background should be allowed to govern themselves within a single nation state.

Proportional representation An electoral system in which parties gain seats in proportion to the number of votes cast for them. It is therefore very difficult for a single party to gain a majority (i.e. 51 per cent of the vote).

Protective tariffs Taxes placed on imported goods to protect native produce.

Protectorate A state that is controlled and protected by another.

Protocols Draft of terms of agreement.

Providence The protective care of God or nature.

Pseudo-scientific Falsely considered to be scientific.

Punitive Extremely severe.

Purges Literally removal by cleansing, but in Stalin's regime the killing of people considered to be enemies.

Putsch A violent uprising.

Radar A system for detecting objects by means of radio waves. In this context, a method of air defence.

Raison d'état What was best for the state.

Rapprochement Resumption of harmonious relations.

Ratify To confirm an agreement formally, to give it validity.

Red Army The name given to the army of the Soviet Union.

Reichstag **fire** The burning of the *Reichstag* in February 1933, an act which the Nazis blamed on the Communists and which enabled them to arrest and restrict opponents in the election campaign.

Remilitarisation Soldiers being sent back into an area where they had been banned.

Reparation Compensation for war damage.

Revanchist Revengeful.

Revisionism The process of re-examining existing interpretations, usually rejecting them.

Revisionist demands This refers to Germany's wish to revise the Paris Peace Settlement.

Revisionist Wishing to re-examine, alter and correct something.

Right-wing military faction A group of ultra-conservative army officers.

Röhm Crisis This refers to the 'Night of the Long Knives', 30 June 1934, when Hitler eliminated Ernst Röhm, a potential rival and leader of the SA.

Rome–Berlin Axis A series of understandings agreed between Nazi Germany and Fascist Italy in 1936.

Rump Czech state The small Czech state – or 'rump' – left over after partition.

SA *Sturmabteilung*, 'storm division'; the Nazi Party's paramilitary force founded in 1921.

Saarland This area, rich in mineral resources, particularly coal, was taken from Germany and administered by the League of Nations for 15 years after the Treaty of Versailles, prior to a plebiscite.

Sanctions Military or economic penalties imposed to coerce a state to conform to international agreement.

Sanhedrin Highest Jewish council in ancient Jerusalem.

Satellite In this case, a small country nominally independent, but controlled by or dependent on another.

Second and Third Reichs Reich means empire in German. The Second refers to Germany between 1871 and 1918; the Third refers to Hitler's Germany 1933–45.

September Programme   A set of war aims drawn up by the German Chancellor Bethmann Hollweg in September 1914, which envisaged annexations to create a German-dominated middle Europe.

Slav   Member of a group of peoples in central and eastern Europe.

Social Darwinism   The theory that ethnic groups are subject to the same Darwinian laws of natural selection as are plants and animals.

Socialism in one country   Socialism was meant to be a world-wide system, but when world revolution did not occur after 1917, Stalin decided it would be possible to build a socialist society in one country, i.e. the USSR.

Socialist   A person who believes that the means of production, distribution and exchange should be regulated or owned by the community as a whole.

Soviet Union   The Communist state that emerged from the Russian Empire after the revolution of 1917. The full title was the Union of Soviet Socialist Republics – the USSR for short.

Spanish Civil War   The conflict between Nationalists and Republicans fought in Spain between 1936 and 1939.

Sphere of influence   The claimed or recognised area of a state's interests.

Status quo   The existing state of affairs.

Sudetenland   An area in the north-west part of Czechoslovakia that contained Czech border defences and which, as part of the Austro-Hungarian Empire prior to 1919, had never been part of Germany.

Table Talk   A collection of stenographic notes which purport to record some of Hitler's private conversations between 1941 and 1944.

Teuton   Ancient northern European tribe, i.e. German.

Third Republic   The republican regime in France between the fall of Napoleon III in 1870 and the German occupation of 1940.

Thirty-Year Rule   Secret government documents are made available to the public after 30 years. So, in 1968 documents for 1938 were accessible.

Top brass   A colloquial expression for the highest ranking officers, ministers, etc.

Transitional book   This refers to the idea that a book went part-way to changing our view, by embracing a middle way between the old view and an emerging new view.

Treaty of Brest-Litovsk   Imposed on Russia in March 1918 whereby a vast amount of Russian territory was annexed, albeit for a short time, including Poland and Lithuania.

Ultimatum   Final demand, with the threat of hostile action if rejected.

Unilaterally   Done by or affecting one person or group or country, etc. and not another.

Va banque   An expression referring to gambling against the banker, i.e. against the odds.

Wall Street Crash   The collapse of prices on the New York Stock Exchange in October 1929.

Wal-Wal   A skirmish at an oasis 80 km inside Abyssinia where the Italians had set up a garrison, claiming the area to be Italian territory.

War of attrition   A war in which one side wins by gradually wearing down the other with repeated attacks, etc.

Washington and London naval treaties   The Washington naval agreement was signed in 1922 by Britain, the USA, Japan and others to restrict the size of navies.

Whitehall   A street in London where many government offices are located; hence a name for the British government.

Wilson's 14 Points   A peace programme put forward by Woodrow Wilson, the US President, in January 1918.

Young Plan   A revised repayment schedule published in 1929 which reduced Germany's reparations burden from £6.6 billion to £2 billion.

Index